PLAYING THE
GAME

PLAYING THE
GAME

LIFE AND POLITICS IN PAPUA NEW GUINEA

JULIUS CHAN

First published 2016 by University of Queensland Press
PO Box 6042, St Lucia, Queensland 4067 Australia

www.uqp.com.au
uqp@uqp.uq.edu.au

Cover design by Luke Causby/Blue Cork
Chapter title illustration by Kymba. The bird of paradise is the national bird of
Papua New Guinea and features on the country's coat of arms and flag.
Map of Papua New Guinea by MAPgraphics
Typeset in 12.5/16 pt Adobe Garamond by Post Pre-press Group, Brisbane
Printed in Australia by McPherson's Printing Group

Cataloguing-in-Publication Data entry is available
from the National Library of Australia
http://catalogue.nla.gov.au

ISBN
978 0 7022 5397 3 (pbk)
978 0 7022 5702 5 (pdf)
978 0 7022 5703 2 (epub)
978 0 7022 5704 9 (kindle)

University of Queensland Press uses papers that are natural, renewable and
recyclable products made from wood grown in sustainable forests. The logging
and manufacturing processes conform to the environmental regulations of the
country of origin.

I dedicate this book to the memory of my parents, Miriam Tinkoris of Nokon, New Ireland, Papua New Guinea, and Chin Pak of Taishan, Guangdong Province, China, who both graciously endured countless challenges and gave their children the best they had.

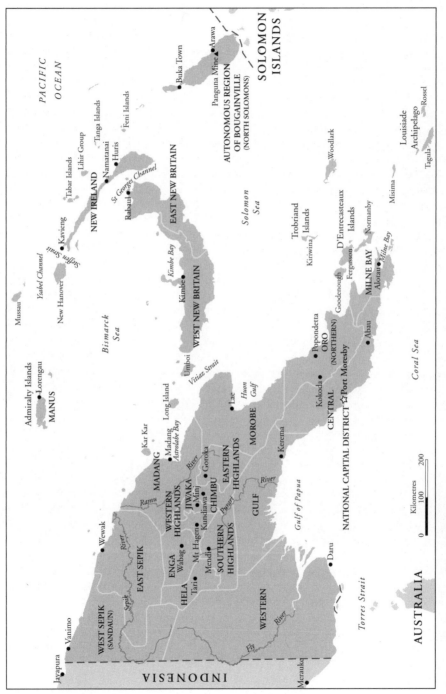

MAP OF PAPUA NEW GUINEA

CHAPTER 1

*When I look out across the sea I think of the destiny
of the unknown. It is to that world of adventure
that we all must go, even though we cannot see what
might lie ahead, whether it will be victory or defeat.*

I was born on the eve of the Second World War in August 1939 on
the Catholic mission of Tanga Island in the Bismarck Archipelago,
New Ireland Province, and named after a local man who my
parents admired, a half-German sea captain called Julius Lundin.
As was customary, my placenta was buried under a *buk buk* tree,
a type of local apple. Many years after I began my political career,
the people on Tanga decided to mark the place of my birth, and
they laid a plaque under the tree. It was a symbolic gesture, a way
for the people on the island to say, 'You can go anywhere, but
physically and earthly wise, this is where you belong.'

My mother, Miriam Tinkoris, was a native of New Ireland,
which was then part of the Australian-controlled Trust Territory
of New Guinea. My father, Chin Pak, was a migrant from
China, and I was the fifth born of their seven children, of which
six survived to adulthood – Agnes, John, Amelia, Louisa, me,
Michael and Joseph. The Cantonese version of my Chinese name
is Chan Chung Man, which means 'straight', like a pillar of the

community. We could probably have had the surname Chin, like my father, but he decided to use the Hong Kong Cantonese version, Chan, instead.

In 1920 Australia had been given a mandate by the League of Nations to rule the northeastern half of the territory, formerly called German New Guinea, which included New Britain and New Ireland. German New Guinea had been a protectorate until 1914, when it fell to Australian forces following the outbreak of the First World War.

In January 1942, while we were still living on Tanga Island, the Japanese invaded the main administrative centre of Rabaul in neighbouring New Britain and established its military base there. When the Pacific campaign of the Second World War began, I became a war child and the course of my life changed.

While I spent my very early years on Tanga, I was only a little boy, too young to absorb the language and certainly not old enough to have any memories. When I was aged three, my family was forced by the Japanese to move to the mainland of New Ireland. Apparently they were suspicious that my father had been involved in the escape of some Australians from their Japanese captors, which would have violated their rule at the time. Our family was also classified as 'foreigners', and even my mother would have been included in this group due to her marriage. Many years later my father told me that the Japanese soldiers who took us by barge to the mainland sat me in the front at the steering wheel.

'That was probably a symbol that one day you were going to lead,' he said.

My father never shared the experiences he went through during the war. I know he definitely feared the Japanese – as with many others, they treated him pretty harshly at times and forced him to carry heavy loads of materials to help make bridges and roads. For some of the war we lived near Namatanai on the east coast of New Ireland, staying with my father's friends, a Chinese and Filipino family, at Rabulut plantation, which was owned by a generation of migrants who came to Papua New Guinea before my father.

The local people would help us when we had to hide in an underground tunnel to escape the American planes on a bombing run. I had a carrier, Buak, whose job was to care for me and take me to the shelter. One day he was not able to reach me in time – someone else took me into the tunnel and I was saved. Buak was killed on the spot, when a bullet went right through the coconut tree he was hiding behind. Although my mother and father spoke very little about him, there was something about his name and the particulars of his death that has never left me.

We had a baby brother, Joseph, who was about four or five months old during this time and he died, I believe, not of external wounds or illness but of shock and fear. It was something my mother felt very guilty about. She was a soft and timid woman and every time there was a bombing raid she was especially frightened and thought that this had somehow been transmitted to the baby and caused his death. On the day they buried Joseph I have a memory of a little green bird, a dove that used to hum in this particular place. Even to this day, whenever I hear the humming or singing of that bird I think of my little brother and the place where he is buried.

We spent the last months of the war at a prisoner-of-war camp, Didiman, located on a large flat area inland from Namatanai. The Japanese soldiers could monitor this open space easily and stop people from running away. I do not know whether they gathered everybody there because they were preparing to shoot us, then bulldoze and bury our bodies, but perhaps the war ended before they could do that. As far as I was aware, the Japanese were reasonable and kinder in their treatment of the majority of the local people than often thought. They had the attitude that they did not need to worry too much about us Kanakas as long as we were not creating any disturbances. They were far more worried about American raids and the longer-term outcome of the war. In our minds, the forces that did the most damage were the Allies – they bombed the islands constantly.

After the Japanese army captured Rabaul, they used the area as a base to advance towards the capital, Port Moresby, on the mainland of Papua New Guinea, where some of the most infamous battles of the war were fought – the most well known being the Kokoda Track, where the Australians forced the Japanese to retreat north over the mountains. Many years ago I went for a walk in Huris, New Ireland, to look at the abandoned Japanese guns on the plateau known as Manmantinut. That was when I decided I wanted to live there. Manmantinut, which is about 100 metres above sea level, means 'a place for a lookout'. It was from here that the local people looked across to Tanga Island – if they saw a canoe with a sail, known as a *mon*, they would start to walk down to the beach and by the time they arrived the *mon* would be there. The Japanese had built a massive runway known as Borpop Airfield on the kunai grass valley below the plateau. I had to remove several undetonated bombs from the area when I built my home and there are probably still more unexploded devices in the bush.

My mother's traditional land is near to my home at Huris. She came from Nokon village on the east coast of New Ireland. The two clans that settled in Nokon and Huris were migrants to the area from further north, distinguished by two birds. One is an eagle, the Maningulai, which is my clan, and the other is a seabird called Tarangau. My mother's language is called Susurunga and the languages in Tanga and Namatanai are different again. Some of the languages in this area carry a similar identity because they share the same roots, for example, Tanga Island and Anir Island – also known as Feni – although separate, might share the same word to describe an object. I can understand Susurunga more than I can speak it.

In New Ireland, all land is passed down through the matrilineal line, which means that I can live on customary clan land, but I cannot pass it down to my kids because I did not marry a woman from that area. In the matrilineal system, a mother must give permission for land to be passed on. For example, she might say to her children, 'This is our clan's land and it is up to you to express your interest in a particular piece.' If she gives consent for her children to live there, no one will dispute it. She would not have to demarcate the land or enforce it legally, because everyone knows that she has the authority of custom, a system that has been handed down for generations.

I do not know a great deal about my mother's early history, but I do know that young girls had to preserve their virginity before they got married. She had to go into what they called a *karuka*, a special house for young women where she was kept for a short period to discourage her from getting involved with anybody. My mother's family was, like most Papua New Guinean families, very close-knit. The Methodist Church had penetrated New Ireland quite deeply but in certain parts there were little hamlets of Catholics. The whole of Namatanai down to where my mother came from was Methodist, and all of her brothers ended up as Methodist pastors and missionaries. I was particularly close to her eldest brother, my Uncle Sam, for whom I had enormous respect. As the eldest of my mother's siblings, whatever he said we would follow. After Sam came Rongtui, Emmanuel Ladi and Malum. Emmanuel Ladi was a pioneer pastor in what later became known as the Uniting Church. He was the first man from New Ireland, in fact from any coastal area, to go to the Southern Highlands of Papua New Guinea and he became very well known. All of my mother's brothers are buried at Nokon.

My father, Chin Pak, was born in the late 1890s in Taishan, Guangdong Province, China. I have been to the village where my father grew up and even went to the house he used to live in. The family had been in the shipping business in China and had reached a certain status in life because of it. My father's eldest brother, Chin Him, had been the first of the family to migrate to Rabaul with some friends but how they got to Papua New Guinea is still a mystery. Eventually my uncle became a maritime skipper, and was known as 'The Captain' or 'Captain Him'. Another older brother, Chan Chung, was supposed to follow The Captain but he did not want to leave China and so my father decided to take his place.

My father would have been about 22 years old when he left his homeland and travelled to Macau, a place he often talked about. He may even have gone to Hong Kong, where his family had a flat on the Kowloon side. After several months he eventually arrived in Rabaul in about 1920, with the goal to find a place to make a living. He did not talk too much about his early experiences in Papua New Guinea – by the time we came along, this part of his life was old news. I believe my father began working as a tailor. It would have been the easiest thing for him to do because everybody needed clothes in Rabaul and he had no other profession. Chinese have always been very business-minded people, creating all kinds of small enterprises and using traditional bartering systems.

From there, around 1921, I understand another distant Chinese relative asked my father to go to Himau in New Ireland to build a coconut plantation. This was where he met my mother, as her village was not far away. It might have been difficult for them to communicate at first as my father spoke Cantonese with perhaps a little Tok Pisin (Pidgin), while my mother spoke mostly in her own language, Susurunga. She was very smart, though, and was eventually fluent in several languages: Cantonese, Taishanese, Tok Pisin, Tanga, Susurunga and others. There would have been a bride price exchange but probably no more than a bag of rice because my father was not a rich person. I do not know what kind of marriage ceremony they went through.

My father told me how difficult it was to establish the plantation, as they had to turn virgin bush into productive land. He had to make everything himself and learn from scratch. It was very arduous because they had only a long iron saw to cut trees like the pandanus and the calophyllum, which are very strong hardwoods. When planting, he would line up the coconuts with a triangular-structured mesh and later told me that I could go and stand in any position in the plantation and the rows would be straight. He was very proud as he had never been trained for that kind of work – he had never even seen coconuts in China.

After Himau, my parents went to Tanga Island to establish another plantation, which is where I was born. The plantation at Tanga is still in our family today; however, the size has reduced from the 70 hectares (170 acres) we used to have because I gave 20 hectares to the church to build a high school, which opened in 2014. For people on an island who are short of land it was a very big thing. I no longer have a house on Tanga, although I used to when the plantation was productive – when labour and freight costs went up it made a lot of remote areas completely uneconomic. Over time, my land there will return to the people.

Essentially I was born between two cultures, and there was a clash in the way that my parents raised us. Although New Ireland was matrilineal, in the sense that land was passed down through the female line, I was dominated strongly by my father's side. My father – whom we called Papa – was quite a serious person and very disciplined. The Chinese are peculiar people in that they want to dominate and have fixed ideas about the way life should be. His view was that when a Chinese boy grows up he should be the head of the family and therefore be honest and hard working. Papa wanted to train us in a certain way so he always spoke to us in Chinese, rarely in Pidgin. If one of us was disobedient – often this was Louisa as she was more temperamental – he would mark a ring in the sand and say, 'Okay, you stay there and do not move. If you move out of the ring then you get it.' Louisa would leave the ring and she would be belted with a stick.

My mother would be the one to comfort us. Her attitude was typical among Melanesians, as she had been brought up to be very thoughtful and accommodating. Papua New Guineans have a particular gift for caring and my mother's influence came from her kindness, generosity and passion. She would give away the best thing in the house to an unexpected guest – even if that meant we might be short of a good dinner. I am told that one time a patrolling Australian *Kiap* ('district officer' – Kiap is a derivation of the German word *Kapitan*, which arose when northeastern Papua New Guinea was a German colony) came to visit my family and my father invited him to stay for a meal. My mother was a little ashamed because all they had were tins of fish, bully beef and rice.

'It is not what you offer, just give the best you can,' my father said. His attitude was that the size of the meal was not important and flavour was not the issue – if you were offering hospitality, you should share the finest that you had. The Kiap, who had walked a long way that day, probably thought he had had a great dinner with Chin Pak's family.

CHAPTER 2

I have often reflected on some of the events over which I had no real control but which changed the course of my life.

There was a definite racial hierarchy in Papua New Guinea at the time I was growing up. The Chinese had whiter skin, which meant they were closer in looks to the Europeans, who were the bosses. Even though my father was an outsider, my mother's family was accepting of him, and very proud that she had married somebody with lighter coloured skin. Because of her marriage, instead of living in a kunai grass hut, she lived in a house with an iron roof and a door, ate with a spoon, fork and knife, and was able to clothe herself a little bit better than otherwise. Within her family, she would have had more authority by virtue of her association with my father.

Chinese people similar to my father's age and standing, however, looked down on him for, as they saw it, going so low as to marry a black woman. There was a view that because my father married my mother, everything he did would be second-rate. Consequently, when the Chinese community had parties, my mother would not be invited. Because of this, many years later, when I became a Member of Parliament, I made a point of taking my mother with me wherever she wanted to go. My uncle Chin Him had also married a black woman, Tin Marliun from Samo village, near Nokon, which brought our families much closer. But my uncle's marriage did not affect him as adversely as my father's because of his personality and his higher standing in the community due to his respected profession.

As a very young child I had no idea that these tensions existed, although as I got older that changed – I knew I looked different and I felt different. Later, I realised that because I was in between two cultures, it meant I had the opportunity to be both. My father wanted to make sure that we were given the same chances as everyone else. He told us constantly, 'You've got to work harder because this situation exists,' and he instilled in us the feeling that we would have to work very hard just to be equal.

While my father was building the plantation at Himau, he built a timber ship, an 85-footer, something he taught himself to do. Himau has no passage and no anchorage so how he did it I will never know. He told me he had to get a special kind of timber for the bow of the ship, as it had to be strong with a natural curve. The first ship he made was called *Kwong Chow*, an alternative spelling of Guangzhou. The *Kwong Chow* was subsequently used for the evacuation of Rabaul in 1937, the first volcanic disaster of that century. It was also used a great deal in my uncle's shipping ventures and sometimes my father would go to places like Tanga, Lihir and Tabar, where my family had some Chinese friends on plantations. Even then, Tabar was talked about as an island of gold, long before the enormous mine on nearby Lihir was developed.

During the war the *Kwong Chow* was commandeered by the Japanese off the Duke of York islands – these islands form part of the Bismark Archipelago and are close to East New Britain. They believed my uncle Chin Him was using it to help Allied forces escape. Apparently the Japanese had found a flag on the ship – it could have been an Australian or a Kuomintang flag, as Chiang Kai-shek was the leader of the Republic of China at this time and was widely revered by many Chinese – and it made them suspicious. My uncle was tortured to reveal information and they used a technique called waterboarding, where they kept him on his back while repeatedly filling his mouth with water and almost drowning him. They kept him on the islands for the remainder of the war and thankfully he survived, although the boat was destroyed and sunk.

As the captain of a boat, my uncle was firm but cool and able to adapt to the changing conditions at sea. My father was not a good sailor at all and, even though he was very fit, was not really the kind of man who was made for the sea. He was better at running the business. My uncle was the definite boss and my father deferred to him; the line of discipline was very clear. Physically there was also a big difference between them. My uncle was a big man who was also more affable, more open, more liked. He loved to celebrate, drink whisky and brandy, and eat lots of food – it was all part of his larger-than-life Chinese character. My father, by contrast, was not much of a drinker at all and he ate a very healthy diet and was slim. These were the same differences between my cousin Joe Chan and me – I am more reserved, whereas Joe was much more outgoing like his father.

Up to the age of about ten, I did not receive any formal schooling. We did not need it – no one needed to count to survive in the bush. We spent our days catching fish, playing and enjoying ourselves. I was close to all my siblings, particularly

Amelia, who was about eight years older than me. Life was very free in those days; there was little urgency and no fixed timeframe to get things done. All we needed to know was how to look after ourselves. I remember going for a swim one day, to an area where there was a sharp reef, and I cut my chest. Of the few medicines available, we had Mercurochrome and iodine – the fastest way to treat infections but not the most comfortable. These were also used when I got sores on my feet because I had no shoes and was walking through mud.

On another occasion, we were staying at Rabulut plantation and my sisters went down to look at a small swampy river, which was not flowing, and they saw some excreta floating on the water. I wanted to have a look at it and fell in and was nearly drowned – they had to jump in and rescue me. But in those days everyone seemed to know exactly what to do when there was an accident or illness. My parents both came from cultures that had relied on traditional medicines for thousands of years and they cared for us according to those customs. Despite all the strife we got into, we survived.

I vaguely remember the end of the war because of a prominent Australian soldier by the name of Robinson. He was the person who escorted all the people in Didiman Namatanai compound to Rabaul on a barge. The Japanese had held Rabaul until they surrendered in August 1945. The Australians wanted all the Chinese families to move to care centres in Rabaul and, once we arrived, we decided to stay on permanently. If the Second World War had not come to Papua New Guinea, I would have grown up on Tanga and I would probably still be there on that beautiful island. The war forced us out of New Ireland and then many years later the volcanic eruption of 1994 forced us out of Rabaul. There have been many situations where I was compelled to respond to events outside my control, to make decisions based on the immediate circumstances at the time.

In Rabaul we lived with Chin Him's family in a very small house with a canvas roof and, even though it had a dirt floor and could be very dusty, it was kept clean. There were a total of four adults and thirteen children and we slept in beds made of wood attached to the posts of the house. It was crowded but we did not mind sharing and sleeping next to one another. We became a very tight family unit and lived in this house for a long time. Gradually we built a wooden house next to the existing one and in 1958 the family moved into the new, properly built house with an iron roof.

If we were lucky we might have had a kerosene lamp to light but normally it would be completely dark by six o'clock. At night the adults would tell us ghost stories – they probably did so to discipline us but I was particularly frightened by these tales. When I could not see, I had the feeling that someone might come and grab me. If we saw a glow-fly lighting up, someone would say that it might be a ghost, or if a dog barked and the sky began to darken in a particular way that meant someone was dying. I was a very fearful child and these stories scared me a lot – a trait I inherited from my mother – and I found it difficult to sleep by myself. My mother would not walk out into the dark, as she would think there were ghosts all around and I took her very seriously. I grew up like her, believing that ghosts exist in darkness and that you cannot see them.

In my mother's culture there was a belief that when someone died they had been poisoned or cursed. When this happened a secret group would come together in order to discover the truth. They might drink herbs or eat plenty of *buai* (betel nut) – then they would hold a stick and it would point to the person responsible.

Perhaps that person had not actually done anything, but he might have wished harm on the person who had died, spat ginger in a certain way, or smoked *brus* (bush tobacco) in a ritual to make it happen. People would be frightened and think, 'That guy, he's got the power with him.' In English you would call it telepathy of the mind but when it comes to PNG culture, it is real. It is a belief that endures to this day.

Another example of this way of thinking arose when I developed asthma. My mother's brother told me I had to take some medicine from a plant grown near the sea that he mixed in a certain way, perhaps with traditional prayers. After I drank it he told me I was not allowed to eat red emperor and surprisingly the asthma cleared up immediately. But six months afterwards I began to think that perhaps my uncle was wrong. The red fish were the easiest to catch because they were dumb – they had big mouths and loved to take the bait. I was a young boy so I decided to simply ignore his instructions. Within days my asthma came back even worse than before. My uncle, who was very reluctant to help me because I had disobeyed his order, made me another drink.

'Now, you are not allowed to eat red emperor but you are also not allowed to eat trevally. If you ask me why I cannot tell you,' he said. I knew if I disobeyed him that the lustre of that medicine might not work. I observed the bans, and I have never had asthma again.

After the war, there were several Japanese ships that had been wrecked in Rabaul harbour, just sitting in the water. We would go out and explore on top of them, and if we felt like it we would sit and fish off the sides. We used any string that we could lay our hands on, found hooks and made our own sinkers by boiling old batteries full of lead. When the lead was liquefied we poured it into a pawpaw branch and it would come out as a line, which we would then chop up with a pair of pliers.

It never dawned on me that people might have died inside these ships. Not too many people talked about that. On the coastal road between Rabaul and Kokopo was the wreck of a Japanese crane and hundreds of tunnels that the Japanese used to hide in with their equipment when the Allied forces were bombing. In the tunnels were submarines, barges and ammunition – some of the equipment is still there today, rusting. It is a ghostly area. Talk was very rife: 'Oh, I came back from Kokopo last night and I heard the footsteps of the Japanese soldiers, marching,' someone would say. Even to this day when I go past there, I think about the soldiers' footsteps and how they'll never go away. Up and down, up and down. These are some of the memorable things that have stayed with me all my life.

In 1950 my uncle Chin Him died in a car accident. He had been driving his jeep in Rabaul and was hit at a crossing by another car owned by JL Chipper, an Australian who had become well off after the war. I believe he was known as 'Hydraulic Jack'. Chipper had not been driving the car himself – one of his staff was responsible – but afterwards we felt that he was something of an enemy to my family because his car had taken my uncle's life. After his death we sometimes used to hear drops of water coming from the rain tank and falling into a bucket – that was interpreted as the sound of my uncle's footsteps. This story had a great impact on my young mind. The sound would frighten me and I would not be able to sleep. Even today, every time I hear water dripping, particularly at night, I think of my uncle, the ghost walking in the house.

CHAPTER 3

*I was good at athletics and very conscious that I
had to be either as good if not better than the others.
I think the spirit of healthy competition naturally
grew inside me.*

The biggest impact of my uncle's death was that my father now
had thirteen children to look after. Some of my cousins, who were
about three or four years older than me, had never been to school
and my father had to take responsibility for them. I was about
ten or eleven when I began my formal education at the Sacred
Heart Catholic School in Rabaul. I went there because I had
been baptised as a Catholic on Tanga. My mother was actually
a Methodist and my father, I presume, had followed some kind
of Buddhist teachings. When they were much older, both my
parents were converted to the Catholic faith by Father Bernard
Franke, our family priest. They never questioned the religious
factor of my upbringing.

Initially two Chinese lay teachers taught us but later Australian
and German nuns and Marist brothers stepped in. The Chinese
lay teachers had not been trained – they had just come to help in
the kindergarten. I was quite old when I went to prep but even I
could see that the quality of education then was very, very low.

Some of the Catholic sisters indoctrinated us with their faith's ideas and said we should change our lifestyle. I was at the age where I just went along with everybody else but I do not think anybody really knew what the sisters or the brothers were talking about. I remember they were not nice or kind to me – they were strict and I suffered some caning on my hands for playing around, or giggling with the fellow next to me.

Being a Catholic meant we saw the other religions as enemies of the church. I knew that to get to Heaven I had to be a baptised Catholic, otherwise I would go to Purgatory, and Hell was not a place I ever wanted to go. When we looked at other churches we would think, 'Oh, those people, they're just no-hopers, really. They can't belong and they'll never get to Heaven.' I thought all these things even though my mother's family was Methodist, that's how strongly we were moulded.

By this age I only spoke Cantonese, Tok Pisin and some of my mother's language, Susurunga. I did not speak English at all until I started school. The whole family was caught in an education gap and we had to try and catch up to the age level in our classes, which was not always easy. My cousin Joe Chan was three years older than me but initially we were in the same class. It was great to develop new friendships, but to be friends with another Chinese or Papua New Guinean kid then was just ordinary. As not all the Australian kids were sent away to boarding school, to be able to sit next to and be friends with an Australian boy was really thought to be something.

While academically it could be hard, sport was a different story. Joe and I were prominent in soccer and basketball, which gave us respect. We formed a team with other Catholic kids and played games against the Methodists. I was a naturally good sportsman and when we did acrobatics I was better than most of my peers.

All of my family, possibly because of our mixed blood, somehow built up very sporty physiques.

Joe and I became altar boys and it was very exciting to be able to ring the bells, although this enthusiasm was more a matter of competition with other boys than a passion for the Catholic faith. It was fun going to Mass as it enabled us to ride bicycles to get there. Joe would serve as an altar boy and then go out to steal mangoes and do naughty, flamboyant things. If there were ever any adventures, Joe would be organising them. Our life in Rabaul was carefree.

The township has an interesting history. Rabaul had been the headquarters of German New Guinea until the British captured it during the First World War. The town had been designed and built by the Germans, and was really well laid out. It was probably the best-designed town in Papua New Guinea. A lot of the houses had been properly surveyed and there were road links everywhere. It was a very friendly place to live. After the First World War it became the capital of the Australian-mandated Territory of New Guinea.

When I was growing up there were many Chinese, Malays, Germans, Ambonese and Australians and a lot of mixed-race families. There could have been up to 30,000 Chinese in Rabaul at that time while the Europeans were the most dominant group. When the Australians started arriving, they began reserving the higher, more prestigious sections of town to live in. Our house was very close to the road to the airport, which was about three miles (five kilometres) away. The area where we lived would have been classified as Chinatown. We had the Ambonese Club right next to us, the Kuomintang Club was on the sportsground and a mixture of racial groups lived around there. There were also rows of Chinese stores. But we seemed to just all live together, mixed up in our areas. By comparison, Port Moresby, which is now the national capital, was segregated along racial lines and quite backward.

By the time I started school I had not seen my older brother, John, for many years. In those days, the best the Chinese could do, especially men like my father who were isolated from their culture, was to enable their children to learn English. A decision was made before the beginning of the Second World War to send my brother and his cousin back to Hong Kong to study as my father's family still had an apartment there. John would have been about seven or eight years old. Not long after he arrived, he disappeared.

For many years we heard nothing and the whole family presumed John had died. The true story was very different. He had been staying with my grandmother when the Japanese started invading in 1941. A close friend of the family persuaded her to allow him to take John out of Hong Kong, promising to look after him. But he took John, put him on a train and sold him as a slave in rural China.

At the time there was a civil war between the National People's Party, the Kuomintang under the leadership of Chiang Kai-shek, and the Communist Party of China run by Mao Tse-tung. Mao, the founding father of the People's Republic of China, had helped to set up the Red Army and their aim was not only to defeat the Kuomintang but also to win over the hearts of the Chinese. When Mao came to power he tried to ingratiate himself with the people using a different approach, by being more communist. When the Kuomintang went through the countryside, no food would be left, they would have eaten all of it. However, when the communist soldiers went through, people would see new crops growing. That was how Mao won the hearts and minds of the people – by doing things, being close to them, helping them in community work. This strategy enabled the ultimate victory of Mao's peasant revolution.

John just happened to be a dark boy of about seventeen in the middle of all this. As the Red Army was moving through the area where John was working as a labourer, one of the senior officers recognised that he did not belong there. He gave John the job of polishing his boots, carrying his gun, and later helped him get on a truck to Hong Kong. When John arrived back in that city after so many years away, he said the only thing he could remember was a particular church, and from there he made his way to my grandmother's house.

In 1950 a message came to us from Hong Kong saying, 'We have found your son.' My father, who was not an educated person at all, had taught himself to read and write so when the letters arrived, all in Chinese, he was able to tell my mother that John was alive.

'Not until I see him and touch him will I then believe it,' she said.

Eventually John arrived home when he was about nineteen years old. My parents were incredibly emotional to see him but I did not get sentimental because I did not remember him. I felt slightly more frightened of him, even though I knew we were related.

John had a difficult time adjusting to life in Rabaul. He brought back nothing, no possessions or skills, apart from the experience of having his hands in the mud. His life in China had been so limited he could probably tell the entire story of his time there in about ten minutes. The life he'd been living was so different from ours and he had a hard time with my father, who was an exacting type of person. When my father wanted something done, John just could not do it because he had never calculated figures or cut a piece of material. John seemed, by comparison to the rest of the family, very dumb because we were able to count and we knew our ABC. As well, John's attitude to the family was condescending as he thought our culture unsophisticated. We did not know that he felt that everybody else was looking down on him. As a result he got on very badly, even with my mother. He once swore at her, as he'd never had to deal with a black woman telling him what to do.

It was decided that John should attend school and he ended up in the year above me even though he was an adult by then. He was naturally bright and a determined person. I remember he would sit up late at night with a kerosene lamp teaching himself to read and write in Chinese and English. He was able to teach himself to do things such as play musical instruments like the mouth organ, a little Chinese banjo and the Chinese piano. He even learned to play a trumpet.

After a while he decided to return to Hong Kong and eventually became a self-made man, working for the Belgian Bank in Hong Kong. One of his wives was very smart and beautiful, good at martial arts, and an executive in charge of one of the prisons in Hong Kong. John learned five Chinese dialects and he could also write them down in a very stylish manner – although my father said his writing was like looking at a crab trying to walk. John's learning came from an earlier time when people expressed themselves differently; the way they wrote was related to the flow of a river or the description of a war. If you asked a modern-day Chinese person to read something that was written a long time ago they might be able to read it but they could not go deeper into the explanation of the particular work. John would be able to interpret it. He was highly knowledgeable, very intelligent.

John's a good man to spend time with, as he is open. He should be wealthy but he's not. He likes the good life – good food, a bit of gambling and has had a lot of girlfriends. He has friends from all walks of life. He is still a citizen of Papua New Guinea but he condemns the political uncertainty, corruption, abuse of power and all the tribal killings. I call him 'The Prodigal Son'. The years when he was lost were very dull and difficult for him but they made a man out of him and gave him a strong determination to survive and succeed.

Not long after John's return, there was another unexpected and significant change in our family. My father's Chinese wife, Yee Kun Chin, arrived in Rabaul with their son, my half-brother, Bosco, who was about seventeen years old. I do not remember whether I even knew of their existence before they arrived but I certainly knew I was not supposed to openly question such matters – I did not know how many wives a person should have. I was simply told that this was my stepmother. In Papua New Guinea men often have children to partners other than their wives and in China it was also not unusual. Papua New Guineans behave in a really human way – they do not see things the way Westerners do. They love kids and they don't really care how you get them.

I could sense the arrival of my stepmother was hard for my mother, though. My stepmother could be quite artificial while my mother was genuine, and she did not know how else to be favourable to my father except by doing her best. My mother and my stepmother tried not to bother each other – they did not argue openly but they probably swore at each other in their hearts. I noticed a certain amount of tension in the way both women served my father and how they both tried to ingratiate themselves. For example, when it came to food I imagine my stepmother was quite condescending towards my mother, as she would have regarded herself as coming from a more advanced culture. In her world, food was something that had to be planned so there would be enough for the next day. My mother was from a completely different environment – in Papua New Guinea there was always a feeling of plenty when it came to foods such as coconuts and galip nuts. The customary way of doing things was quite lavish and when you ate, you ate it all, you didn't save any for later.

Bosco had been born in the year between the birth of my oldest sister, Agnes, and my older brother, John. After Agnes was born, my father returned briefly to China where Yee Kun Chin fell pregnant with Bosco. I do not know whether my mother was aware of this at the time. When John was born he was given the name Cheng Meng, to mean 'the real son'. This was a way for my father to let his Chinese wife know that he also regarded John as his legitimate son. Bosco's arrival in Papua New Guinea was, of course, at my father's wish, as he wanted him to go to school in Australia. Shortly after his arrival he was sent to St Augustine's in Cairns. Later he went to live in Sydney and once or twice we went there to visit him.

I discovered much later that my father also had another Chinese wife – his first, in fact – called Ne Kun, whom I never met. They had one daughter, my half-sister, Chen Shen Mei. Chen Shen Mei was a beautiful woman. After she married and became pregnant something went wrong during the birth and she became disabled. The child, a son, survived and later moved to Australia. I have met him many times, although we are not particularly close.

It was in the 1970s, when I first went to Hong Kong, that I first met Chen Shen Mei. She was completely paralysed from the waist down and was being cared for by her husband and another relative. To meet her was an opportunity to reflect on my own life and to admire how she had survived. Chen Shen Mei was forever radiant, forever smiling and never talked about her problems. She would always ask, 'How are you? What are you doing?' Perhaps this approach helped her to escape from the discomfort she was in. I found seeing her quite uplifting because she was so positive. As Hong Kong developed they looked after disabled people a lot better – I got her a wheelchair so she could move around more easily and enjoy a little bit of life.

In Rabaul, some of the well-off Chinese families were sending their kids to Australia to be educated at places like St Joseph's in Hunters Hill, Sydney, or Chevalier College in Bowral in country New South Wales. They often came back smarter, faster and able to talk about rugby football, and I wanted to be like them. When the opportunity came up for my cousin Joe and I to go to Marist College Ashgrove in Brisbane, we accepted. My sister Louisa was sent to St Scholastica's in Sydney and eventually became a nurse, but Agnes and Amelia were too old for school by then so they missed out.

We felt very sad to be leaving our families but there were other girls and boys going to different schools in Australia at the same time. When we left Rabaul in early 1954 we got stranded in Lae for about a week as the Skymaster, a DC3, had some technical problems. We had to stay in the Qantas staff house, where we shared our feelings of being away from home. I was fourteen years old and this was my first significant adventure. Those few days in Lae enabled us to build a feeling of independence and a sense of resilience.

When the plane arrived in Brisbane, we were met by a senior student, Daniel Tufui, a Tongan in his last year. He had not gone home for the holidays, as he did not have enough money. When we looked at him we said, 'Oh, he's of the same skin,' and that lifted our spirits a lot. Daniel accompanied Joe and I to Ashgrove, where we had several days to settle into our new school before the other students arrived. Daniel was a great footballer and we talked about rugby a lot. All these experiences gave us a feeling that there was a chance we might be able to fit in to our new life in Australia and gain some respect from all these 'whities'.

Chapter 4

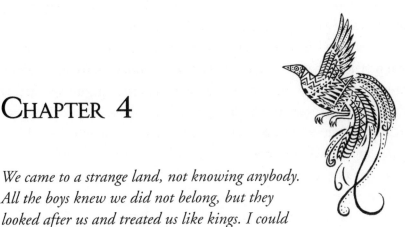

*We came to a strange land, not knowing anybody.
All the boys knew we did not belong, but they
looked after us and treated us like kings. I could
not have found a better place to grow up.*

The years I spent at Marist College Ashgrove were probably the best years of my life. I knew well before I went to Australia that this was a white man's country and we were strangers in it. The Marist brothers did not give us any special treatment, nor were they especially sympathetic, but ironically this gave us the confidence to believe that we would survive in a completely new environment. We had so many new things, such as our own beds and mattresses, along with a higher material quality of life than at home. This helped erase any feeling that we had something to feel sorry about.

I was probably homesick for the first two weeks and I certainly missed my mother because she was so gentle and kind. It was good to get away from my father's strictness, though. Of course, I was grateful to him too because he worked very hard to get Joe and me into Ashgrove. I do not believe we were subsidised at all as scholarships did not exist at that time and the fees would have been about £120 a year. Even if scholarships had existed, it was rooted in our family not to seek out help but to do things for ourselves.

When the other boys arrived they treated us very well, and it was not long before we felt very much at home. Two years later, more mixed-race Papua New Guineans came to join us. It was possible that some of the Australian kids did not like us but we made a point of not doing anything to upset people – that was never in our temperament, anyway. If there was hostility towards us it was not openly expressed and there were very few problems in that regard.

My view was that I had not come to challenge anyone or impose my way of life on the situation. I had come to belong. This was quite easy for Joe and I to do because we had always led a fluid lifestyle. As children we'd had to adjust to the circumstances – if we had rice, we ate rice, and if we had potatoes, we ate potatoes. While other students used to complain, the food at the school was so much superior to what we were used to. For me it was outstanding: bacon, eggs, jam, up to a dozen slices of bread with just a little butter, and my favourite food, liver and gravy. That was a banquet.

I had gone straight into Grade 8 at Ashgrove but I felt handicapped, as I did not have a good general education. I had to work hard to keep up, particularly in English, although in mathematics, Latin and French I was on par with my counterparts. The Australians talked a different language, much more aggressive and 'fair dinkum'. I had the languages of Tanga, Namatanai, Susurunga, Pidgin and Tolai, but as I became more and more involved in English the old languages were pushed out.

I did get into trouble sometimes – perhaps because I was not paying attention or was talking or giggling – and I would be caned on my hands. I tried to be different and a bit cheeky, but at the same time basically follow the rules. If I was able to do something funny and the Marist brothers could not find out it was me, then I had one up my sleeve, a little victory of some kind. But I did not dare to toy with the things my friends were doing; they smoked and swore and I did not.

My father had very clear expectations of how we were to behave. When he said something we listened. One thing he told me before we left home was that I should not play rugby; however, rugby was my passion. The teams in those days were organised according to weight – they had more brains at that time – and I was in the 7-stone (45-kilogram) team for two years. After that I jumped up straight into the first grade. I was disobeying my father but as he was so far away I did not think he would find out. During one match I both broke and dislocated my shoulder and I was in a cast for several weeks with my whole arm sticking out. I was frightened of my father's reaction so I did not tell him.

The First XV at Ashgrove was regarded as incredibly important and we were given special treatment, such as steak before the games. I represented the First XV for three years and the team remained undefeated for nineteen years. It was a school that produced a lot of footballers. John Eales was an Ashgrove boy, as was Des Connor, who became one of the best rugby halfbacks in the world. I believe I am still in the school's Hall of Fame today.

Joe and I often stayed with our classmates' families during the holidays because we did not have anywhere else to go. We only got to return home twice during our time at Ashgrove as it cost about £150 for a round trip from Rabaul to Brisbane. I was very close to the other boarders, many of them rural kids. One of the families we stayed with was the Allen family at Currumbin on the Gold Coast. My friends came from places like Canungra or from cane-cutting families in Bundaberg. They were the boys who, like me, had to leave their families to go to school and we had a lot more in common with them than we did with the dayboys.

I was really good friends with one boy, Peter Demartini from Proserpine. My friends and I would do everything together and we spoke a common language. We used to get two shillings on the weekends and if we went to the movies we'd still have a shilling and sixpence left to buy a drink and an ice cream. If we did not have enough money our friends, who were very generous, would share what they had. Once at cadet training camp it was terribly cold, and so Peter came and slept by my side so we shared six blankets instead of having three each. At other times we joined the Marist brothers at the junior college in Mount Tamborine or we went to O'Reilly's Guesthouse on the Lamington Plateau. Joe, who was by now a bit too old for school, hiked every day we were at O'Reilly's for about 20 kilometres and swam in the river.

Joe left school by Grade 10 as he was by then about eighteen years old. He was really just interested in having a great time – you could call him an extrovert – getting involved in sport, singing, going out, that was his game. For all of those years at Ashgrove we did not meet many girls or women and there were no female teachers. Mr Boothby, who was the chef at Ashgrove, had two daughters, who occupied a very special place in our school life. This was the first time I had seen blonde European girls up close – they were a little bit older than us. For us to see a tall, blonde woman who was pretty – that was really something. We did get a chance to meet girls at the end-of-year socials with schools like All Hallows'. While I was a very shy person Joe Chan would be on the dance floor – he was very forward with the girls, very jovial.

As I spent these formative years in Australia, I missed out on many of the traditional feasts and rituals back home, such as pig killing and death ceremonies. I was not part of customary preparations in New Ireland where the young men would leave the village, be isolated and fast, and then dance with the *tubuan* or *dukduk*. The *tubuan* is a spiritual and earthly spirit for which the young men had to perform quite a number of sacrifices. They would be on a special diet so they could perform a spiritual dance and walk over fire; they would take the human, physical sensation out of themselves. One of the boys would have to dress up as the *tubuan*. His mask and costume were made out of bush materials and weighed a lot – you had to be very strong to wear them. The young men would behave as if they were psyched up, out of this life, and everybody around them would be singing and beating the drums. The *tubuan* brought with it the spirit of the ancestors to energise people and wipe away all the bad omens and, for us, this was equivalent to a Pope's blessing.

The way I grew up, my surroundings, the food I ate, the muumuus, the feasting, dancing and way of being were always Papua New Guinean. The Chinese side of me was only dominant on certain occasions. As a consequence, I became very good at adjusting to the environment I was in. When I was at Ashgrove I was exposed to many new aspects of culture and my mind became more and more compartmentalised. I became someone who was happy to venture into different areas, to be able to open up a new world for future generations. It was not something that was calculated, it was simply the way I was brought up – to be adventurous, to score the try, and to do it differently.

Chapter 5

'He's a black man. How can they allow him to come and stay here?'

I finished senior school in 1958 and the following year I went to the St Lucia campus of the University of Queensland to study agricultural science. I chose this area of study because it was knowledge that I could take home; I could use it to grow better coconuts and learn about how to deal with diseases in the plantations. However I had only been at university for about six months when I had an accident, and the course of my life was changed once again.

Apart from telling me I should not play football, my father had also forbidden me to ride a motorbike. Having independent transport, however, was important at that time, so I ignored his command and bought a Bantam motorbike for about £80 with the money I had been given for rent. One morning on a very rainy day, I was riding my motorbike and my wheel got caught in the tramlines at Toowong. I was riding through a cutting when I was tossed off my bike and hit the rock wall, severely jarring the bones in my back and damaging some discs. I had not been wearing a helmet but fortunately I did not suffer any serious head injuries. I ended up at the general hospital and initially the doctor said he did not think I had broken anything and suggested I should go home. As soon as I tried to stand up, though, I just collapsed.

'Oh, you'd better stay here and get checked out,' he then told me.

In those days there were very few orthopaedic surgeons and even though the X-ray showed everything was in place it seemed my only option was to stay very still with a cast around my body. After several weeks at the hospital, they shifted me to Greenslopes, a former hospital for recuperating soldiers. Here I had to learn to walk again, like a child, with just a few steps at a time. I did not tell my father about this accident but my sister told him what had happened.

'You've disobeyed me, you have to come home,' was my father's message to me.

Even though I wanted to finish my studies, I had missed too many sessions and it appeared likely I would have to repeat the year. My father would not talk to me and refused to send me any more money. The accident had already robbed me of the opportunity to be selected to play for the Australian Colts, for which I was being considered as a halfback for the under 19s against the All Blacks. But I was very determined to stay and complete my studies, and so I talked to the university and organised to work as a general labourer at Gatton Agricultural College, about halfway between Brisbane and Toowoomba, for the Christmas holidays. I needed to survive without my father's help and see if he would cave in to what I wanted.

One of my tasks at Gatton was to sit at the back of a tractor piling hay and tying up the bales; other jobs included ploughing potatoes, milking cows and carrying bags of chook dung, which was incredibly compact, heavy and smelled terrible. I found getting up at five o'clock in the morning was okay, even though it was cold, and I could manage everything I was asked to do except standing out in the hot sun. After about three months, though, I had to make a choice. Communication was poor at Gatton as there were no telephones but I knew my father was determined not to send me any more money. He was very fixed and would not change his mind. Eventually I felt I had no choice but to return to Papua New Guinea because I knew I could not survive without his support.

When I returned to Rabaul, I decided to stay for only a short period. I still wanted to better myself and, even if I could not go to university, I wanted to learn. The only way to get business experience at the time was through the co-operative movement that was pivotal in PNG government and business, and so I applied for a position in the public service based in Port Moresby. I was employed in the second division, which was an equivalent level to all the Australians. I think when they saw the name Chan they assumed I was Chinese and let me in on the basis of that.

Moving to Port Moresby was difficult. I was dark and the city was dominated by whites. As soon as I arrived I began to feel the impact of discrimination. At first I was accommodated in a donga at 4 Mile, the neighbourhood where all the Australians stayed. The manager of the unit was immediately unhappy to see me and although he did not say it directly, he told several others, 'He's a black man. How can they allow him to come and stay here?' The next day I was kicked out. I went straight away to see my boss, John Keith McCarthy, the Director of Native Affairs, who was close to Dr John Gunther, the Assistant Administrator of Services.

'This is my officer of the second division,' McCarthy told Gunther, 'and he should be allowed to stay there.'

'All right,' replied Gunther, who was an open-minded fellow. 'Well, he was kicked out of there so let's not put him back. Let's put him in the modern accommodation at Ranaguri in Konedobu.'

This was also a hostel full of white men – Australians and Europeans – but it was much more spacious with individual rooms. The British manager, Mr Coffey, put me in a room directly above him and if I dropped anything he would tap on the ceiling with his umbrella to remind me not to make any noise.

It was difficult. I never made any friends as I felt the other men were biased against me and they were also older than me. I would go to the mess and they would sit on one side of the room, eating and drinking together, and I would just sit at a table by myself. This went on for months. One night, an Englishman by the name of Bill Onslow, who was a Health Extension Officer, came up to me after dinner.

'Where are you going?' he asked.

'I am going back to my room.'

'Why don't we go to the Kone Club?'

I was shaking at the thought but I told myself, 'I have got to break through this barrier somehow.' Onslow was a big guy, very tall, and I thought, 'Well, if anything happens he will look after me.'

When we arrived he asked me if I wanted a beer. I did not drink but I told him I would have one. He got the drinks and brought them back to our table, and the manager of the Kone Club noticed me and called Onslow over. I could see by his reaction that Onslow could not believe what he was hearing. He then told me we would leave after we finished our beers. I could sense there was tension. On the way out I asked him if everything was all right.

'Yes, everything's fine,' he replied.

Later, Onslow told me the manager had said, 'You'd better finish that beer and get that bastard out of here.' But Onslow suggested that there had not been a problem with me, it was just that I was not a member of the club. I knew that was not the real reason.

I decided to go and see Harry Jackman, the Registrar of Co-operative Societies, who was my immediate boss, and I told him I had been kicked out of the Kone Club because I was not a member.

'That is not a problem,' Jackman told me. 'I'll recommend you.' He and Joe Lynch, the Legislative Draftsman, and McCarthy all supported my application but I was rejected. In protest, all three men resigned their membership. The matter was then taken up by Percy Chatterton, who was a member of the Legislative Council and an English missionary. He spoke out very strongly and the newspapers took up the issue. The episode marked perhaps one of the first public debates about racial discrimination in Papua New Guinea.

I began my life as a public servant as an audit trainee in the Co-operative Section of the Department of Native Affairs. The co-operative movement was the starting stone of all forms of businesses in Papua New Guinea and originated from the fact that the advisors for the Australian government tried to mobilise the clan and tribal system to encourage common economic needs. There were quite a few businesses involved in the early co-operative system and they marketed produce, like copra for instance, and helped to distribute it. Each business had its own association and the growers would sell their produce to their local co-operative society, who became the buyer and distributor. The co-operative movement was a very practical approach to helping educate people about business at their own level; it was a way to translate the idea of development in a very real sense because everyone was given an opportunity to participate.

Initially I was just a bag carrier for Cedric Johns, who was the Senior Audit Inspection Officer, and my boss under John Cruikshank, the Chief Inspector of Co-operatives. Papua New Guinea at this time had been divided into nineteen districts – these eventually became the provinces – each with its own white District Commissioner, who were appointed by the Administrator and regarded as gods with multiple responsibilities in law, policing and public administration. If they made a decision it would be final, with no appeal. Cedric Johns was a very hard-working and dedicated man, a heavy smoker, who was a natural auditor and a good person for me to learn from. He was patient and he taught me the basics of the accounting systems of the co-operative movement.

I was very keen to learn so I read a lot of books and later corresponded with some colleges in Australia. A co-operative society can only operate with very honest people. All the receipts and invoices had to match up so that when the co-operative society made a profit, the money could be redistributed as dividends back to the people. I started my training at the Co-operative Education Centre at Konedobu. Another Papua New Guinean there was Elliot Elijah, who later became closely involved with the Pangu Party. Pangu was regarded in its early days as quite a radical party, an aggressive political grouping with strong ideals. The co-operative system fitted in with it as its philosophy was neither individual nor social – but somewhere in between.

Cedric Johns and I travelled a great deal for work to places I had never been, such as the Sepik region, Madang and the

Highlands. All the Australians I worked with became great friends; we went out on patrols and camped together and I never had any problems with them. In about 1962, I was asked to lead a delegation of six experienced Papua New Guinean co-operative officers to Nasinu College in Fiji. Perhaps the administration felt I was broken in because of my experiences and thought that it would be advantageous for me to learn more.

We stayed in Fiji for six months under the leadership of the United Nations Food and Agriculture Organization (FAO) with the South Pacific Commission also involved. One of our teachers was an Indian, Mr Ramarnurthy, and I was deeply struck by his intelligence. When someone asked a question it was like a game of ping-pong, with the answer coming back from him as quickly as the question was put, and it was filled with detail about the principles, history and practical aspects of the co-operative movement.

When the training in Fiji ended I was sent to Gulf Province for several months – this was when all officers learned the very real, down-to-earth realities of helping co-operatives to grow. I was then given another great opportunity and offered a scholarship to a college in the United Kingdom. But when the offer came to go to London I knew I couldn't accept it as there would be no one to look after the family. Instead the opportunity was given to Tore Lokoloko. Many years later, I convinced Lokoloko to become the second Governor-General of Papua New Guinea, replacing John Guise.

For some time I had become increasingly aware that my father needed help to run the shipping business. My father was still paying school fees for my brother Michael and another of my uncle's children. To do this he was running a little 40-foot boat ferrying copra back and forth between Rabaul and New Ireland,

and carrying cargo to all the plantations. I did not realise until much later how difficult it had been for him to be in business as he spoke mostly Cantonese and a little Tok Pisin, and the only way he socialised with other Chinese was to gamble a little. The shipping industry was highly competitive, and socialising with others was a large part of establishing contacts and securing more business. My father was handicapped all his life by these limitations and as he was getting older he was also getting sick more frequently. It became clear that someone had to go back to Rabaul and take more responsibility for the business. I decided to be that person.

Even though I was an adult, my father was still an important figure of authority and doing something he didn't approve of was difficult. Straight after college I had taken up smoking, sometimes up to a packet of Peter Stuyvesant a day and the occasional Camel cigarette. My father knew about this and he strongly disapproved; however, rather than telling me directly he made his point in a much more powerful way. Whenever he walked into my little hut office I would immediately hide all my cigarettes. Without saying anything, anything at all, he would simply place a packet of cigarettes on my desk and leave it there. It was a very powerful way of him saying, 'I know you are lying to me.'

It was clear that my father, whose motto was obedience, honesty and discipline, had formed the view that I was defying him and that hurt me terribly. It was a punishment of the moral kind.

Chapter 6

When the boat left the harbour we would say goodbye like in a myth. We had no communication, no way of knowing what was waiting out on the open sea.

Before I arrived, Joe had already come back to Rabaul and was employed in the family business. He was very fit so shipping suited him – he could run around all day as long as he did not have to sit down and write anything. The company had originally been named after the 40-footer boat, the *Sepik*, which my father had bought from an Australian living in Kavieng. Later I named the business the Coastal Shipping Company. When we started, the *Sepik* was probably doing about fifteen to twenty trips every month – we decided to increase this to a daily trip because we had to be more competitive to survive.

It took six hours to get to New Ireland from Rabaul. The *Sepik* would come in at about three o'clock in the afternoon and we would then discharge the cargo, reload, and take off again at midnight, arriving at six o'clock the next morning on the west coast of New Ireland. The captain of the boat had no formal training; he was a local man who knew the oceans and had been a seafarer for many years. He used a compass and a kerosene lamp at night to navigate through the islands over the reefs. We did not have radar so no one could tell – until it was too late – what might be underneath the boat. We were very lucky and only had a few accidents over the years, especially northwest of Baining in East New Britain, which was notorious for heavy seas.

Later we expanded to a 50-footer boat and then an 80-footer, and eventually we ended up with the *Gerard*, a 120-foot, three-masted schooner that could carry almost 2800 bags of copra. The ship had been built in Kiel, Germany, in 1921 and used to run between Western Australia, Adelaide and Sydney carrying wheat.

Until Independence in 1975, all PNG laws were administered by Australia. The Legislative Council of Papua and New Guinea governed until 1964, when it was replaced by the House of Assembly. Around the early 1960s new laws stated that any boat over 50 tonnes had to have a properly qualified captain. This meant the local people we employed no longer qualified, as they could not write much more than their own names. So we had to hire Australians because they had the right certificates. However, most of the waterfront captains and engineers were drunks – they were probably bums at home, which is why they had ended up in Rabaul.

One of the Australian captains, McKay, was very capable; he could sail single-handedly. My mother used to look after Captain McKay, and at first she cooked him a beautiful steak for dinner but he would not touch it. The only thing he would eat was raw meat. So she offered it uncooked with a few slices of bread and he would eat it, just like that, like a hamburger. It was his idea to change our three-masted schooner into a one-masted schooner, as no one else really knew how to handle a ship with such complex rigging. He just chopped two of the masts out.

The *Gerard*, under the command of another captain, once ran aground on an island. The boat was refloated without much damage – luckily, because of its soft iron plating. Some of the Australian engineers we hired could be quite heavy drinkers, especially those who had come back from fighting in the Korean or Vietnam wars and had metal plates in their skulls. One war veteran was quite immobile most of the time – he would have whisky for breakfast, lunch and dinner along with whatever he was eating. We called him Dr Diesel and he was really something. We had to carry him on board, take him to his cabin and tell him not to touch anything, and then the boat would be run by a local mechanic.

I was working very long hours. I was the clerk, the manager, the driver, the cargo boy, the messenger and the copra carrier. I had to learn to be the accountant as well, to raise my own invoices. I would have to send letters away, to start working out the bill of lading, and then go to the wharf when I was needed. There were no forklifts, slings or mechanical equipment – it was all manpower. When the ship came alongside we would have to go down into the hold and carry up to a hundred bags of copra, which weighed around 80 kilograms each. Once we had brought the copra out onto the deck and then onto the wharf, we would have to carry it onto the back of a truck. The boats often left Rabaul at midnight and once they had departed I would come home. One memory that will always remain with me was arriving home and finding my mother waiting up for me. She would keep rice and whatever pot of food she had ready and sleep on the table until I returned. She was that kind of a woman.

Sometimes I would go out to the plantations. The boats were slow, only travelling at about 7 knots (13 kilometres per hour), and I would throw a string and catch a lot of fish. We always carried rice on board and cooked the fish in salt water. In those moments, out on the sea, it was a beautiful, simple life. But for the first two years I worked really hard and was often too flaked out to think of anything else apart from the occasional game of rugby. It was largely due to my workload that I waited for a while before I started thinking about getting married.

I met Stella Julietta Ahmat in 1964 when I was 25 and she had come to work in Rabaul in a Chinese retail shop, Pings, which was about a five-minute walk from my house. I had met other women before but they were mostly infatuations and nothing came of those encounters. Stella was very pretty, of mixed heritage that included Malay, Chinese, Spanish, Filipino and Papua New Guinean. Her mother had a conservative attitude and wanted Stella to marry a European man because quite a few mixed-race girls in Rabaul had married Australians. For some families the dark-skinned men were not that popular and so I was looked at with suspicion.

By then, because of my experiences in Port Moresby, I accepted such opposition and was quite undaunted by it. I knew that if there was a choice between a European man and me, there was no real choice for Stella, as he would get the first call. Even though I had been close to other women before, I wanted to be closer to Stella. While her mother, Rita, was not too keen on me and her older brothers were a little distant, Stella's stepfather, Sam Moessner, who was a mixed-race Papua New Guinean and German, was more open. Stella's real father, Mali Ahmat, had been a mixed-race Papua New Guinean and Malayan and had died during the war when her mother was six months pregnant with Stella.

It was partly because of her mother's attitude that I felt pushed to prove something. My upbringing had taught me that if there was a mountain to climb I must go up it, if there was a hurdle to jump, I must cross it. It was a challenge for me to win Stella and to prove to her parents that I could do it, that I was good enough. In the end she chose me, the dark-skinned man.

We were married in 1966 in one of the biggest weddings ever in Rabaul. There were probably 500 people who came to the wedding in the Catholic Church in Malaguna, with a huge reception afterwards at the Rabaul Kuomintang Hall. We were married by Father Bernard Franke, the German priest who had converted both my parents to Catholicism. Father Franke was very close to our family for many years. For me this was an opportunity to also do something for my family as they had been treated with such condescension for so long, and the wedding showed everyone that we were able to do exactly what other people did.

A year later, on 19 July 1967, our first child, Vanessa, was born. She was very close to me from the beginning and, even though I felt I could look after her on my own, if she started to cry I began to panic. Most of the time Stella looked after her or we would get the house girl to help. I was always fearful to look after babies and even to this day I still do not know how to do it. As soon as Vanessa was born I started to call her 'my princess', and was so proud to be a father for the first time.

After Stella and I married we stayed at Warramung, a plantation on Anir (Feni) Island, with its owner, an Australian Second World War coastwatcher called Ray Lacey. I had come to know Ray through our shipping business. He was a very kind person and also an alcoholic – he would be out cold by seven o'clock every evening. While he was drinking, Ray would often yell for his young cook, who would come and pour beer down his throat. Soon after Ray would be fast asleep. At three o'clock the following morning, Ray would wake up completely on the ball, and within minutes he would be out on his motorbike. If I decided to go with him, I would hang on to him tight and we would travel along a very tricky road he was building around the island. He eventually created a 35-mile (56-kilometre) ring road, all made by him, his tractor and the people. It was an incredible achievement.

Another Australian character I met at this time was Graeme Carson, whose father Lewis owned the freehold for more than 50 islands on the twin atolls that made up Nuguria. They were the atolls north of New Ireland, and were very beautiful. The Carsons had built an airstrip on Tekani Island and when the Minister for External Territories, Bill Morrison, arrived for a visit in 1974, he was able to touch down there and then come across to Anir. I took him all around the whole island in a Volkswagen Beetle. The Nuguria plantation is now closed but it used to be very productive in terms of locally harvested copra.

People like Ray and Graeme were highly active in their adopted communities, building roads and airstrips, and helping to run the local councils. It was not long before it was suggested that I might make a good local member for Namatanai Open, New Ireland, in the House of Assembly. I think they believed in me because the shipping business was already bringing change to the islands, as there was now a regular, reliable service. People were able to produce goods to sell, and they knew they would get their cargo and their medicines. I think some people thought, 'This is the guy, this is the man.'

The House of Assembly had appointed members and they were also beginning to introduce elected members, like my good friend Wally Lussick, who also joined the second House of Assembly in 1968 as Regional Member for Manus and New Ireland. Quite a number of elected members were Australians, such as Jim Grose, who had been a big planter. Up to this point, politics had never really interested me – I did not have a clue what a representative was even supposed to do. The idea of running for the seat of Namatanai troubled me initially as I had left there during the war but, having worked in government, I began to think about how I could help to continue to build roads or bring in air services. It was this idea that gave me some motivation to start considering contesting the election.

As I was debating whether to stand, another memory from my time as a co-operative officer in Port Moresby played a part in my thinking. John Guise was a mixed-race politician and already, by 1961, was a member of the Legislative Council and a highly effective indigenous leader. He really knew how to play the political game and was one of the few mixed-race people who had a licence to drink in Papua. In those days you could not drink in Port Moresby if you were a Fuzzy Wuzzy unless you had a licence. Guise could claim both sides because he was part French.

Once, when I went on patrol on a *lakatoi* (a double-hulled boat) around Central Province, I heard that John Guise would be visiting the Aroma Coast and I went along to see him. The excitement in the air was so strong I began to think that someone was coming from a celestial space. I stayed on the edge of the crowd to watch Guise arriving ashore on a dinghy. He was a tall, bald, impressive man wearing a long black coat and sporting a big moustache and, when he stepped off the boat, the crowd reacted as though it was the arrival of the Messiah. He was a special creature – he knew how to read and manipulate the mood of the people. Without pausing, he walked straight to the church so he could preach, giving the impression that he was close to the hierarchy of the church, perhaps even more important than the Bishop himself. I was too far away to genuflect before him but I probably would have done so.

John Guise played a vital role later on as Deputy Chief Minister, Speaker of the House of Assembly and as the country's first Governor-General. He was a long-time supporter of Independence and pro the Pangu Party's views. Seeing John Guise made a big impression on me. I wondered if I too could represent the people with everyone adoring me, if I could be another John Guise.

One night at Ray Lacey's Warramung plantation, quite a lot of elderly clan leaders gathered and we sat together until after midnight, talking and drinking whisky. They were the main producers in the area and Ray gave them a lot of support to help get their businesses running. They were really keen on regular shipping timetables and we often talked about how to service their needs. They were still operating at quite a basic level – I vividly recall it sometimes took five minutes for them to sign their name on a cheque but, as Ray was the man behind them, they always had money. They were all the big, big boys and I had to respect them.

I still had not decided whether I should contest the election and worried that I did not really know enough. However, my mother's village Nokon was in that district and so I had a strong sense of connection to the area through her. Somehow, that night I finally told everyone that I had made a decision: 'All right, I'll do it.'

At that time people had very modest expectations of what an elected member could provide them, but of course they looked for opportunities to make life easier. No one wanted to be a millionaire, but if they could buy a tractor it would mean they would not have to carry everything. They were just thinking about sustaining themselves for the rest of their lives. Mostly they were content and what they did not have they did not ask for.

Many years later, when Papua New Guinea had developed more, it was the people living in the towns who made the most noise. They saw other people driving, drinking and eating new foods and that created jealousy and demands for better housing, better medical care and so on. Back then, though, the majority of people I was dealing with were used to a particular way of life and they demanded very little, if anything. There are still many, many Papua New Guineans like this today. Their needs are simple and their demands are few.

The concerns of people centred on basic survival. Medicine was important at that time but education meant little – if someone became a genius on Anir Island what could they do with it? They probably knew very little of what I talked about, the kind of improvement I was hoping to bring them. I did not say too much about health except to talk about aid posts that I wanted to establish, as I knew that meant a lot to them. Ray Lacey had the control of persuasion of the people of Anir and, while I had his support, I was still concerned about the mainland of New Ireland, which was where Dick Lanzarote stepped in.

Lanzarote's parents had come from the Philippines in 1913 and he was involved in local-level government on the mainland. He was really well known and popular for his contribution to roads and agricultural development south of Namatanai. He probably should have stood for parliament but he had never been to school and felt he was not educated enough. Dick Lanzarote said he would give me his backing. He was a really kind, generous guy and without his support I would not have gone ahead. He had an old Land Rover, left behind by the Australians after the war, and so that was how I got around.

Ray Lacey was very politically astute. He was the one who thought of my campaign slogan, CHAN IS THE MAN, and we printed this on black and yellow posters. That headline was a good quotable quote. I began to tune in to international shortwave radio and listened to programs such as the *Letter from America* by Alistair Cooke. This was the period of the Kennedy years and I learned a great deal about the situation of racial discrimination in the United States. The impact of the black US civil rights campaigner Martin Luther King, Jr did not carry the same weight for me compared to white people making the decision to change. The fact that the white man was prepared to adjust, to provide justice, impressed me greatly.

Organising the elections was a simple process. Everybody was honest in those days; they were fair elections and no one was throwing money around. When people queued up to vote they would just put an 'X' next to the name of the candidate or they would say their name and the officer would record it. The districts were administered very efficiently and professionally by patrol officers or Kiaps, and the Assistant District Officers. People knew very little of what elections were all about; they vaguely understood that we were turning into a more inclusive government, and that elected members would be able to speak on their behalf.

While I could rely on Dick Lanzarote's vehicle on the mainland, I often travelled by boat to all the outlying islands. Wherever one of our ships went I would just hop on and go. Joe and my younger brother, Michael, had by now taken on more responsibility for the shipping business, so I was free to pursue the campaign. I had good opponents, real politicians who had been working with local councils and government who knew the system much better than I did. They were either locals or mixed race. My main opponent was Robert Seeto, a mixed-race Papua New Guinean and Chinese, and one of the first presidents of

49

Namatanai Council. He was a tough man to beat, as he was very popular. I did not have a strategy to beat him. When I decided to stand I just had one thing in mind: I had to win.

The night the results came in, I was listening to Radio Rabaul. When I learned I had won the right to be the representative of the Namatanai electorate of New Ireland district I had a feeling of satisfaction and humility, the same emotions I had at school when we won a football game. My mode of politics was not about improving the administration as the system was already running. Nor was I proposing changes to government so it would be more capable – those things were beyond me. I just thought I could make life easier for the people and give the forgotten parts of Namatanai a proper voice.

CHAPTER 7

*I did not really know much about government,
let alone self-government and independence.
These ideas were far too big for me.*

Members of the House of Assembly were mostly Australians appointed to the roles with a few elected Papua New Guineans like me. This was Australia's first and only experience as a colonial power and they supported the country under the *Papua and New Guinea Act 1949*, which had replaced the *Papua Act 1905* and the *New Guinea Act 1920*, merging the two administrations. The Australians who lived here at that time were a different breed. They generally kept to themselves because they were used to another standard of living, but they performed their duties well.

I was in the second House of Assembly formed in 1968 and my experience during this time was terrific, as the administration was neutral and run by non-politicians who did not offer the kind of favouritism that is more common today. They focussed on policies that bred stability, co-operation, hard work and determination. The original House of Assembly building was quite old and classic, located in downtown Port Moresby.

Alongside it was a three-storeyed timber office, which allowed us enough room to have our own offices. The administration was headed at that time by David Hay and later by Les Johnson.

The House of Assembly was really more of a forum than a parliament. Most of the District Commissioners who were under the direction of the administration were also Australian. Philip Bouraga, who became District Commissioner of East New Britain, was the first dark-skinned man to hold such a position. He went to the Australian School of Pacific Administration (ASOPA) based in Sydney. Bouraga was a top Papua New Guinean at that time and had been closely groomed by Dr John Gunther, the Assistant Administrator of Services in Papua New Guinea. All the Australians who came to Papua New Guinea had to attend courses at ASOPA – they learned about our administrative structures, culture, and the way they ought to conduct themselves.

We were highly dedicated, obedient and knew our duties, and I knew that as a public servant I had to perform. No one had to tell us that we could not participate in politics – there was no conflict of interest. For a long time I was too raw to know what other members were talking about, and I did not have any real say in anything, as I was just too inexperienced. If I was directed by the Administrator to do things I would, or if I had an opportunity to ask questions I would. Gradually I began to understand my role, learned about the rules and all the standing orders, and eventually was able to take on the full role of an elected official.

Members of the House were not given a proper salary, only a small allowance. I stayed with one of my cousins and every day I found my own way to work by bus – there was no transport provided. The Assembly ran very smoothly. Whenever the Speaker said the House was adjourned until a certain date, I would go home to Rabaul and resume working in the shipping business. I rarely stayed in Port Moresby for any longer than I had to – it was a dead town in those days.

As Speaker, John Guise was pretty dictatorial and no one questioned his authority. He looked like a version of a priest in his wig and gown. Everyone believed what he said but looking back he was rarely right – he just called the tune and everybody listened. He actually knew very little about standing orders; he just ran it the way he wanted to run it. Even if we had said anything, he would just have rolled us anyway. John Guise was Speaker until 1972, when Perry Kwan was quickly sworn in because Paul Hasluck, the Governor-General of Australia, was arriving to open the third House of Assembly. Kwan was able to run the opening but thereafter it was beyond him. He lasted only two months in the post, which was then taken up by Barry Holloway. Kwan served as the member for Kavieng Open in New Ireland and he was a one-man show. He was three-quarters Chinese from Kavieng, a real character with long hair. He had a white wig and always wore the same outfit: a long-sleeved white shirt, white trousers, white shoes and a black bow tie. That was how he was even represented on the ballot sheet – they would simply print a picture of a bow tie and people would put a cross next to it. His party was the United Progress Society, which was neither conservative nor progressive. He always had a lot of ideas and he would go to the villages during the campaign and carry a copy of *Time* magazine and talk to the people about what was in it.

During my election campaign in 1972 my car broke down in the middle of the night on the Kavieng to Namatanai road. I had an assistant with me, as I did not travel alone, and as he was fixing the tyre who should come along but Perry Kwan in his utility.

'Oh, you've had a puncture. Okay, do not worry. Go and sit down,' he said. He took out his foldable chair and offered me tea and coffee. He had a hot water bottle, kettle, a thermos flask, as well as some biscuits. We sat on the side of the road enjoying a break while the tyre was changed – it was quite an extraordinary encounter.

It was not too long after I entered the House that I was offered the position of Vice Chairman to the Public Accounts Committee working under Bill Fielding, an Agricultural Officer. The Popondetta cocoa scheme had been established after the Second World War and gave leasehold blocks to Australian ex-servicemen. Bill Fielding had been given a block but the whole venture turned out to be a big flop. Even though the scheme was well organised and well funded, the crops developed dieback disease from an armyworm, and the whole enterprise collapsed.

Bill was a marvellous person – reasonable, patient and well versed in his role in accounts and in all the operations of government. We spent a lot of time looking into the auditor general, the public accounts, and then into all the other departments. I quickly became familiar with all the deliberations and decisions they had made. Sometimes Bill and I would travel together to check on the implementation of different projects and it was during this time that I was given a much broader exposure to the rest of Papua New Guinea and a deeper understanding of the way government actually worked. This was a period when people like Bill were effective, aggressive and committed in the field of public account inspections and reporting. He also resolved many conflicting issues in the public service and rationalised some of the duplication of departments.

We travelled to places in the Highlands like Mount Hagen, Goroka and Kegesugel in Chimbu Province near Mount Wilhelm, the highest point in Papua New Guinea. Kegesugel is about 2700 metres above sea level, and the people there could only grow certain kinds of export crops like pyrethrum, a natural insecticide extracted from dried flowers. One of our roles was to help support new industries, in order to encourage community participation and the fairer distribution of income. Pyrethrum was a completely new crop for Papua New Guinea and had come to us from Kenya, where the majority of its production took place.

We also developed other new crops such as English potato and cardamom. We went to Karimui, also in Chimbu Province, which was pretty flat and sparsely populated. We could not get there by road so we had to fly in to investigate what could be grown in such conditions – about 800 metres above sea level. It was recommended they grow cardamom, as it was a small seed that was not too heavy, which meant it could be flown out at not too much cost in terms of airfreight.

I found this work really interesting. It was not directly related to accounts but about the performance of agriculture and whether or not people were implementing the policies of the government. My impression of the Highlands region at that time was that it was a very peaceful, unassuming society; the drums were not beating too much and if they were there was always a reason for it. Highlanders were a highly disciplined people and while they fought, they did so for a cause – perhaps someone had stolen some pigs, encroached on someone else's land, stolen a woman or married without proper compensation. They were not violent for the sake of it – if an outsider happened to arrive during a tribal fight they would make sure that person was safely removed from the fighting zone so they could continue.

The Kiap system, the controlling mechanisms of government, and even the physical structure of new buildings had a big impact on the people in these remote areas, as did the implementation of public service policies, which were rigidly obeyed. People were generally extremely co-operative. The white man was in charge, he was everything – he was the patrol officer but he was also the magistrate. If someone disobeyed him then they would be considered an outcast. One Kiap who became District Commissioner of the Western Highlands, Tom Ellis, effectively ruled the Highlands. I heard a story about him preparing to open the Mount Hagen Cultural Show one year and the organisers told him they should defer the ceremony as heavy rain was coming. Ellis disagreed and said, 'No, we will launch the show,' and then he went out onto the oval, opened the show, then looked up to the sky.

'Come on down, you bastard!' he shouted, and immediately the rain came down. A lot of Highlanders talked about this, saying, 'That man is God! He controls the rain.'

I gained a great deal of knowledge through working with Bill Fielding but also through meeting entrepreneurial Australians like the millionaire and aviation pioneer Dennis Buchanan. Buchanan was very well off, self-made, and probably owned the biggest aviation business in the southern hemisphere. He had started life as a cargo boy loading aircraft, then went into ticketing and from there he grew to owning more than 50 aircraft through his company Talair. I admired him and I wanted to be like him, and many years later I followed him into the aviation industry. Buchanan was driven more by ambition than greed. There was nothing wrong with that as many people benefitted. I believed it was a natural progression for him to become not just successful, but also strong and in control.

Ron Neville was a Big Man (a commonly used Pidgin term for a traditional leader who has gained authority and respect through community service and the accumulation of wealth), a former Kiap, and an enormous influence in the coffee industry – he was known as 'Mr Coffee'. Neville was also a member of the Public Accounts Committee and the Chairman of Public Works. He would stomp into departments and public servants under investigation would shake. Also, due to his involvement in public works, he understood all the operations relating to roads, bridges and other major infrastructure projects. He brought with him a wealth of experience and knowledge.

Neither of these men gained success overnight – they achieved everything through hard work and they went through some tough times. I respected them as I had also begun my life in business as a cargo boy and I knew how hard it was to be successful. By meeting men like Buchanan and Neville, I could see that they wanted to help build a more robust Papua New Guinea for the benefit of the community as well as their own personal satisfaction. They treated me very well and I cannot pick a time or an incident in which I ever felt offside with them. I would also say that Papua New Guineans in general would have had nothing but respect for them – there was never a sense that they were resented for their success.

Another significant Australian I met during this time was Ken Tresize, who had been a Senior Co-operative Officer in Samarai, Milne Bay. In those days Samarai was a very small island just off the southern tip of the mainland in the China Strait and the headquarters of the whole province. It was where the District Commissioner lived and it was an orderly place with no law and order issues. All the foreign vessels used to pass through the strait and Samarai was able to accommodate these ships. Later on the administrative headquarters of Milne Bay moved to Alotau, as Samarai was just too small.

Tresize was an amazing man of tremendous knowledge – he had no degree but he could match any professor of economics or history in knowledge. Many men like him who had come to Papua New Guinea as Kiaps spent a lot of time reading when their work in the village was done – there was often nothing else for them to do. At one point Tresize returned to Australia but he could not acclimatise to his old life; he felt far more at home in Papua New Guinea as he could speak about three or four local dialects and was used to the lifestyle. He would travel across the globe, hitching lifts and sleeping in a bag, and all was right with the world as long as he had his cigarettes and whisky. He had a lot of local girlfriends but he never got married. He was just not that kind of person.

Tresize became my working mate and when I was appointed Prime Minister he was my speechwriter for many years, and one of the best I have ever come across. When I set up my aviation business in the 1980s he looked after my accounts – in every way he was a treasured, trusted friend to me. When he finally returned to Australia, he lived in Port Douglas initially, but it got too big for him so he moved inland to a town called Mount Molloy, which had one post office, one cop and a little pub. For him it was just right and he was happy there. I visited him there right up until the time he died. We lost a wealth of experience when he left Papua New Guinea – he gave a great deal to me and my country in his own quiet way.

Chapter 8

The world of self-government and independence was an unknown thing, a world we could not see, could not touch. But it was something to fight for.

Overall the colonial government was doing a pretty good job. However there were issues that concerned me, such as land rights and the ownership of resources like fishing and forestry. The discussions in the House of Assembly at that time were more academic in relation to how land should be used, and there were debates that were partly influenced by what was happening in Africa following the end of colonial rule. There were a lot of different voices promoting various philosophies, different approaches.

I had already witnessed some resource and land issues in New Ireland, where my mother was born, and right from the start, from my co-operative days, I believed that if the people had ownership of their own resources they would be more able to develop in the way they wanted. A government does not have a human mind; it cannot know the needs of the people. When I spoke to citizens in my electorate they were in favour of logging, as they did not have to do very much to generate income from this enterprise – the trees were already there. But when I started to look at the unfairness of these deals, I realised I was in a position to change the system. In 1972 I introduced the *Private Dealings Act*, which gave landowners the opportunity to deal directly with the developer without the interference of the state. This was difficult as the colonial government was used to having control over resources and I had to persuade them that the landowners should be the main beneficiaries of any harvest. That law, although passed, was never really implemented and was later repealed.

As the elections for the third House of Assembly approached, questions about the political future of the country became more pressing. The greatest internal push came from the Bully Beef Club, a sophisticated group who had some formal education, and members included Michael Somare, Albert Maori Kiki, Cecil Abel, Peter Lus, Barry Holloway, Paul Lapun and Tony Voutas. An Australian political scientist, Voutas had studied at the Australian National University in Canberra and was highly influential, committed and genuine. This group, which formed the core of the Pangu Party, could see that self-government was the way to go, followed by independence.

In between the Pangu Party and the United Party led by Tei Abal and Mathias Toliman, who were ultra-conservative, were those of us who were neither for nor against self-government, but we wanted the freedom to be progressive. Consequently I founded the People's Progress Party (PPP) with Warren Dutton, a former patrol officer; Daniel Bokup, a teacher and member for Kavieng; Donatus Mola; Louïs Mona; and a former Marist brother from Central Bougainville, Joseph Lui. The PPP brought some great friendships into my political life. I was the father and the PPP was my son; I had to nurse it, develop it and let it grow. Later on we were joined by two outstanding men, Bruce Jephcott and Jim McKinnon, and our network extended throughout the country.

The PPP was an educated group of people who believed that development should be prioritised in terms of agriculture and that massive production could be achieved in this sector. We supported private enterprise, law enforcement and the preservation of religion. Most importantly, we wanted to establish long-term ties and a close relationship with Australia. We had decided that we must have a binding friendship with Australia, which was not difficult because most of us who became members of parliament and administrators had been schooled there. The strength of some of these friendships had grown from our experiences on the sporting fields.

Our approach was to make sure that the Australian government would help us to cross the bridge towards self-government. The wording for the timing of self-government – which was created by the PPP – declared that it 'shall be attained on the 1st December 1973 ... as soon as practicable'. The PPP was like the referee between those who wanted to go too fast and those who were going too slowly. I felt what we were doing was looking beyond the words 'self-government' and 'independence' towards our long-term future and the sustainability of power.

In the 1972 elections, I was voted in again as a member of the PPP. Tei Abal and his United Party were the biggest party in parliament but the PPP formed a coalition government with the National Party and the Pangu Party. Michael Somare became our new Chief Minister, appointed by the Administrator, and I became the Minister for Internal Finance. Albert Maori Kiki was a well-known union man who backed Somare and was probably able to secure a large number of workers' votes at a time when the public service was growing. He became the Foreign Minister. The opposition, due to its size, had a very powerful voice in the Assembly.

The Secretary for Treasury was an Englishman, Harry Ritchie, who came from Fiji. He was a very nice man and being British with experience in the colonies he was highly flexible. He would sit in Cabinet but allowed me, as the elected politician, to say things he could not. He was really more like an advisor, a father figure, who helped guide me through the issues of finance. My attitude in my new role was the same as it had been for everything else I had ever done – it was just another game. I had to play by the rules and if I was fit enough I would succeed. I carried the same view I had developed on the rugby fields at Ashgrove as a young man: I never played to lose.

The United Nations was becoming an increasingly prominent voice in our move towards independence and they began to push Australia – which was just a little peanut country at the time and probably wanted to have a bigger say internationally – towards giving Papua New Guinea its political and economic freedom. From my reading of the situation, and I am not a historian or a political analyst, I thought the greatest push for self-government was really coming from outside the country and influencing people within.

Internationally, the political landscape had been changing for many years, particularly in Africa where several countries had gained independence after decades of colonial rule. People were hearing about Kwame Nkrumah of Ghana, Jomo Kenyatta of Kenya and Julius Nyerere, who became the first President of Tanzania. We heard of people fighting for a cause although we did not realise that people were getting killed in the process. Those facts became more exposed when we started learning about Idi

Amin, who had become President of Uganda in 1971. We had also watched Fiji gain independence from Britain in 1970 under the prime ministership of Ratu Sir Kamisese Mara, a man who was physically imposing and really well respected.

In my view, Fiji started the push towards independence in the Pacific. Fiji had their own currency, buses and cars, and institutions like the college I attended in the 1960s, yet they still had their own customs and retained their tightly knit society. The chiefs were respected, as were the powers of parliament and the democratic institutions. All this superimposed on our thinking – if Papua New Guinea was going to move forward in that direction, Fiji was an excellent model.

Ultimately the decision for self-government, to be followed by full independence, was made by the Australian government headed by Labor Prime Minister Gough Whitlam in late 1972, with the change of government in Canberra. Charles 'Ceb' Barnes, a long-standing Country Party Member of Parliament and the Australian Minister for External Territories from 1963 to 1972 for the previous Liberal Country government, had thought it would take several more years but Whitlam wanted it pushed through faster. The colonial government had some very good people, such as Donald Cleland and Les Johnson, an educationalist and a Labor man, to implement Whitlam's policies. As Ceb Barnes had said we could not have independence unless we were financially sound, a lot of my focus when I took office was on how to create economic stability. The mineral wealth on Bougainville, which already contributed such a substantial part of our revenue, was crucial to take Papua New Guinea towards that transition.

From personal contact, I knew that there were serious fears about the possible change independence would bring for the country. Many people – Highlanders, members of the United Party, people who were mature but less educated – could not interpret the real meaning of self-government or independence. They wanted to know whether there would be improvements in their lives when they reached the destination. In some sections of society there was a great deal of opposition to the move. Josephine Abaijah, the first and only woman elected to the House of Assembly in 1972, started the Papua Besena movement, which wanted Papua, a British protectorate that the Australians had administered from the beginning of the twentieth century, to be completely independent of New Guinea. The educated Papuans did not want to be united with the rest of the country. However, the tide was moving towards a unified country and Josephine Abaijah was fighting like Joan of Arc. Unfortunately, the paternalistic system was too much against her.

There was also substantial opposition to unification by the Mataungan Association based in East New Britain. This was a militant group who wanted a fully autonomous local government. The Tolai people there felt they were superior to the rest of the country – they had people like Oscar Tamur, John Kaputin, Alkan Tololo, Sam Piniau and Ronald Tovue, who were more educated and sophisticated – and believed they would be better off on their own as they already had a strong economic base and enough resources to look after themselves. For a different reason, those from Bougainville identified geographically and ethnically, due to the pigmentation of their skin, as more akin to the Solomon Islands, and had no real desire to continue to be part of Papua New Guinea. There was also the Johnson Cult on New Hanover, which aligned itself with US President Lyndon Johnson and wanted to vote for him and completely break away.

With so many voices calling for different things, one of the main concerns we had was how we were going to unify the country. An important issue that faced the Somare Coalition was the establishment of an independent Constitutional Planning Committee (CPC) to develop our Constitution. All the ideas submitted to the CPC were thought up by academics, lawyers and international experts. The planning committee did a great deal of work, which was then presented to Cabinet for us to debate. By the time it reached parliament we had more or less reached an agreement.

One contentious issue, as far as I was concerned, was the establishment of the Ombudsman Commission and the Leadership Code, which I believe built into the Constitution a view that the elected representatives of the people could not be trusted. I have always been inspired by the Constitutions of other countries, such as the United States, which talked about ideas like all men being created equally – a noble sentiment that makes people feel they have high moral standards to live up to. But our Constitution ended up being partly built on distrust. It came about because some academics and saintly bureaucrats wanted to incorporate clauses in the Constitution to stop greed. African countries were used quite extensively by these experts as benchmarks – perhaps because we were also black – and as African countries were 90 per cent corrupt, there was a view we should be 'looked after' right from the start.

As Finance Minister, I had a say in how much we were prepared to go towards the decentralisation of power. The local government system was already pretty well established because of the Kiap system and we had a fledgling national government. The CPC was pushing for decentralisation, which left a gap for another administrative arm of government, and I was looking at the question of what we could afford. But how would it be possible to split Papua New Guinea, with its diverse languages and geography, into separate states and still function? We conceded we would need to devolve certain powers to the provinces to keep the country together.

By virtue of Bougainville's demands for independence, the decision by government was to go ahead with the Constitution but to make provision for Bougainville to have special status. But once we had given Bougainville greater autonomy, the idea spread throughout the country, which was how we ended up with the provincial government system. This decentralisation of powers was manageable for provinces like Bougainville but in other parts of the country it was a massive change. People who knew absolutely nothing about government were being asked to throw away their spears, sit down at a table and begin to create a more modern society.

The political tide was turning very fast but we had no foundation in the economic area at all – no Central Bank and no currency. Les Johnson said, 'You have a long way to go to catch up. You have got to move.' That was when I had to start working really hard because I knew nothing about banking or what its function was – I did not have a clue.

The Australian Treasurer at the time was Frank Crean, the father of the more recent former Australian Labor politician Simon Crean, and I was in frequent contact with him. On one visit I arrived in Sydney but there were strikes so I could not fly to Canberra to meet with Frank. It took me four hours to get there by road and it was at that meeting that we arranged to take over the Federal Reserve Bank and change it into the Bank of Papua New Guinea. Most of these decisions were made by just Frank Crean and me.

I was just a player and I would be lying if I pretended to be in control of the situation – I do not think anybody was. Only the gods, whichever side they came from, were able to make that bold statement to say we were ready. But ready or not, change was coming.

Chapter 9

The decisive moment in our history came when we established self-government in 1973. It was really just a question of making certain that every machine in the engine room was working in order to get there.

The question of Papua New Guinea's survival was not the main issue as we headed towards independence, as I knew Australia was genuine in its support and would not abandon us. We needed to create all the institutions to ensure we could run a nation. I was learning incredibly fast – I had to take in a lot to familiarise myself with the jargon being used, the language of economics. As Minister for Finance I was still quite ignorant but smart enough to see that I had good people around me, like Australian economist Ross Garnaut. As we got closer to independence I had a pretty good team of expert people in place. Ken Woodward from the University of New England was an advisor, as was Pat Curley, who was very much at the top of the public service, and she was very smart. Somehow I had just the right team of expatriates to help me. While they brought knowledge and experience I was a creator, an instigator. I always have been.

In terms of the process towards the practical implementation and establishment of the Central Bank, they were just as raw as

I was, but they had the brains to say, 'Boom! Yes, we'll do it.' Someone in the team would say, 'Look at the Federal Reserve of the United States … the Reserve Bank of Australia … the United Kingdom … the African countries … New Zealand,' wherever, and from there we were able to mould the kind of *Central Banking Act* that I wanted, one that would embrace the colour and the quality of successful banks around the world. After studying various laws and taking recommendations from the banking committee, we brought in legislation to support the economic system but the introduction of a new currency proved to be a little bit more challenging.

Once again, I didn't have a clue where to start, although I knew that no country had ever gone into independence without its own currency. I gathered people like Henry ToRobert, who became our first Governor of the Bank of Papua New Guinea, and Ross Garnaut together, along with consultants from New Zealand, and we set up a currency working group. Another initiative I was involved with during this period was the establishment of Papua New Guinea's first international loan. Along with Secretary for Treasury Harry Ritchie, I had to go through the steps of calling on people at organisations like Ord Minnett, the Commonwealth Bank, the Bank of New South Wales (now Westpac), and every financial institution in Australia – anyone who had anything to do with money. I had to look the part, wear my tie and coat, and tell people what a reliable country we were. The world needed to hear about this little island of Papua New Guinea that wanted to move further on from where it was.

The international banking institutions were not so sure. At that time, under the *Papua New Guinea Act*, the Commonwealth Bank of Australia automatically guaranteed all our loans. But I wanted to have a stab outside the country, outside of Australia, to get our first loan in our own name but still under the umbrella of the Australian government guarantee. Harry and I, along with Mekere Morauta, who ended up becoming the first PNG Secretary for Finance and later Prime Minister, set out for London, Switzerland and Germany. Eventually I succeeded in establishing our first loan from the Swiss Bank Corporation for five million Swiss francs. Even though the amount was relatively small, the purpose of the loan was to tap into the international market and gain financial standing. The loan was due to be paid back over five years. We paid it back in three, which improved our credit rating. This was the beginning of establishing Papua New Guinea's international credibility.

Aid we were receiving from Australia at the time made up probably about 60 to 70 per cent of our internal revenue and the remainder of our funds came from copper and agricultural exports. For several years we had become used to the Australian dollar – it was what everyone used in the stores to buy foreign goods and the people had learned to rely on it. I wanted to introduce our own currency, one that people would identify with and have confidence in. Thinking about the best way forward on this issue was very much like playing rugby at Ashgrove – at times I had to decide whether I should go alone or pass the ball, whether it would be easier to sidestep or make a try. Those days at the Marist College helped a lot in my role as Finance Minister. It felt like a huge risk but I knew the most important thing was to be decisive.

We chose to call our currency the kina, which would initially have the same value as the Australian dollar. *Kina* was the name of shell money from the coast, which people hung around their necks as something valuable and it was also highly respected in trade with the Highlands. The word *kin* was also in the language of the Western Highlands, and it meant 'a store of wealth'. The working group debated other ideas but eventually we could see that the use of the name kina and its smaller counterpart, the toea – from the name of an arm shell used mainly in Papua for bride price exchanges – could serve to unite the country.

The design of the kina note, which had a pig's head on it, had a lot to do with building confidence. Everyone knew that the pig was the most valuable thing in our culture – it was used in dealings for marriage, land and death, dances and all kinds of traditional ceremonies. The variety we chose was a wild pig with a tusk, which was what Sir Peter Lus wore all the time around his neck in parliament, so it was also symbolic of a chief and his authority. I wanted people to identify with the kina, to know that it was not just as strong as the dollar but better, as it carried traditional images of wealth rather than a picture of the Queen or a white man with a moustache.

The committee also had to consider the lifespan of the kina notes – we knew that most people did not have wallets and that money would be carried in baskets or *bilums* (woven string bags) and get wet in the rain. So we decided to create a kina coin as well, because we knew it would last. I decided that not everything colonial was bad and that it would be good to preserve the old British shillings made for the Territory of New Guinea, which had a hole in the centre. By punching that hole, which was my idea, I saved about $500,000 in its manufacture, because we did not have to use so much copper nickel. The stylised bird of paradise on the coins was specially designed.

The decision to change the currency was met with a lot of fear and a big uproar from people who thought that they would no longer be able to buy goods from Australia. The leader of the Opposition and the United Party, Tei Abal, and many other business people did not trust the new currency I was proposing. They were anxious to confirm that this 'fuzzy wuzzy' bit of paper would still be able to buy imported goods. The policy I adopted – which I do not believe had ever been practised anywhere else in the world – was to have a dual currency period for six months, where the Australian dollar and the PNG kina were interchangeable, and then the dollar would be gradually withdrawn from circulation. The whole purpose of this was to establish a period of time to get the system working, as we did not have the Central Bank fully firing at that time.

The kina and toea were launched on 19 April 1975, six months before Independence. On that day all the ministers were at the Central Bank in downtown Port Moresby when someone arrived with a telegram for me, saying that Stella had given birth to our fourth child, a son. After we had had Vanessa, two boys were born – Byron on 13 June 1969 and Mark on 2 February 1972. Before I could read the telegram – an open piece of paper – it went through the hands of John Guise, who was then the Deputy Chief Minister. When John read it he said, 'Oh! We should call him Toea,' and then passed the telegram on to me. Somehow this news reached Chief Minister Michael Somare, who was just about to give a live radio broadcast to the nation. At the end of his speech he announced, to my surprise, 'The Minister for Finance's wife has just given birth to a baby boy and he shall be known as Toea!' That was how my third son was named.

Stella was in hospital in Rabaul when she heard the announcement and she was initially disappointed and upset. I had not even had the chance to talk to her or explain what had happened as there was no telephone connection. It took me at least a day to get back to Rabaul and before I even got there she was already receiving flowers from people congratulating her on the birth. In the end we were both happy with our son's name and glad he had not been called Kina – a child with a lower denomination can always aspire to be higher. Toea also fitted in well with our family history – the word *toy* in Taishanese and Chinese means 'boy', so it was perfect.

The launch of the new currency was a big day for the country. I feared the reaction of the business houses, wondering if they were saying, 'How can this unknown Julius Chan introduce a new currency? He's never traded foreign currency in his life!' I knew that right across the nation they would just have to trust me, as we were all working in the world of the unknown. And no one initially understood the foreign currency exchange system. Before, anyone travelling to Australia would be able to use their dollars but now they had to put their kina in the bank and convert it into dollars for exchange. Now we were buying the Australian dollar out of the system to form the basis of our foreign currency reserves, which was the agreement I had reached with Frank Crean.

I quietly monitored the movement of the Australian dollar, knowing people were hiding them under their beds or trying to smuggle them out of the country in their shoes and underpants – a huge amount of Australian money was even found in a baby's bassinet. Of course there was a free flow of money out of Papua New Guinea, but that was exactly what I wanted, although I never said so. Six months after the introduction, I revalued the kina against the Australian dollar, raising it by 5 per cent. I told the public there were two ways of introducing the change – go soft, go lower than the Australian dollar as a lot of countries did, or go strong. I said that if I had taken the soft currency approach, imported items would have become very expensive. This was not a currency trick as I explained that inflation was high, oil prices were high, and all these things were impacting on the economy, and so an appreciation of the kina was the right thing to do at the time.

The policy I adopted in terms of the international movement of currencies is as relevant today as it was then. Some people were disappointed because the kina was then above the dollar but others started to have greater confidence in the kina and began to regret keeping all their Australian money. It was at this point that people began to say, 'This Julius Chan, he knows what he's doing.'

This whole period was very exciting and I worked very, very hard. I overexerted myself for several months – there were many long nights of little sleep, trying to catch up, trying to learn my trade. I would take up to five hours to read some documents just to understand what they were talking about while the experts around me could probably do the same in an hour. Consequently, at the end of 1974, I had my first infarction of the heart – a blocked artery. I was just 35 years old.

I had gone down to Sydney with my family at Christmas to stay with my father and stepmother at their house in Earlwood. Because the question of citizenship in Papua New Guinea was still being debated, Australia had opened up its immigration policy to allow most of the foreigners living in Papua New Guinea to move there. There was a mass transit of Asian people who could not claim to be Papua New Guineans who went to Australia, including my father and stepmother, who settled in Sydney. In our family we had to decide who would go with my father and who would stay with my mother. I was definitely on my father's list and I believe my half-brother, Bosco, was too, although I'm not sure who else my father wished to go with him. This was before PNG's Independence in 1975 and I did not take up the opportunity to move, and so I automatically became a citizen at one second past midnight on the eve of Independence. I swore a declaration before the Commissioner for Oaths that I would remain a Papua New Guinean.

My stepmother was happier living in Australia as she could socialise more with Chinese friends and they would often go to Chinatown for lunch. A few of their friends from Rabaul also went to Australia, which created further opportunities for them to acclimatise. My relationship with my stepmother was always cordial. I certainly never put myself in a position where I had to pick a fight with her. I was very loyal to my stepmother because I was loyal to my father and I respected whatever he did, whatever he wanted. My mother, though, remained in Rabaul and she probably missed my father in many ways, but she was a tolerant and contented woman. She was surrounded by her children, who were all incredibly important to her. I do not believe that there was any resentment towards my father – it all seemed quite amicable because my mother was so understanding.

In Sydney I had been playing in the garden with Vanessa and Byron – we were racing each other, as in those old houses the backyards could be up to 30 metres long. All of a sudden I felt short of breath. At first I thought it was just because it was so hot and later I reasoned that it was because I had been exerting myself for so long. However, the intensity of what I was feeling was something completely new to me. Fortunately I had a medical appointment the following day, which had been arranged some time before by Robert Cotton, who had been the Minister for Civil Aviation under William McMahon. Years before, when Robert Cotton and I had been to a meeting in New Caledonia together, I was struck down with malaria. During that time Robert was very caring and arranged for me to stay at the Menzies Hotel before I returned to Port Moresby. When he knew I was coming to Sydney he arranged for me to see his doctor – a professor at a

Sydney hospital – and the day he nominated happened to be the day after my infarct.

Even though I still felt unwell and found it difficult to breathe, I really only went to the doctor to fulfil an obligation to Robert. At the university I met a professor who tested my heart and he immediately told me not to move, that they were taking me to hospital. That was the first time I had ever sat in a wheelchair. I stayed in the hospital for several days until my heart stabilised. The artery had been blocked and, like the bark of a tree, it had healed itself. As the doctors interpreted it, the damaged part had been compensated for by other areas of the heart. I was told there was nothing I could do but to take medication. Robert Cotton helped to save my life because if this had happened in Papua New Guinea things might have been very different.

I was told not to worry about the problem too much but in 2002 it happened again. At that time I was at home in Port Moresby watching a football game and I had had some wine, and I may have had a little bit of whisky too. I must have been on my second or third glass of red wine and I was getting really quite excited by the intensity of the game. I had also tried to do a bit of exercise while watching it, to help me keep fit. All of a sudden I felt slightly dizzy. I tried not to panic but I knew something was wrong – my heart had developed a really fast beat.

By now I knew the danger of heart failure, and I was more anxious than the first time it happened. I went into a shadowy world of clouds. My heart was beating so fast that, had it continued, I probably would have died. I was admitted into intensive care. One of the doctors decided that they had to stop my heart and then start it again. They killed me for a number of seconds, maybe up to a minute, and then kick-started me again.

Luckily my heart went back to normal and I was then placed under observation.

The doctors wanted to organise to have me flown down to Australia on a Medivac flight. Everyone around me seemed quite frightened – at one point even former PNG Prime Minister Paias Wingti popped his head into my room, although I did not get to speak to him. It was then suggested I go to Australia but I refused.

'No, that is not me,' I said. 'If I have to be wheeled, it will only be within my own country. I will never touch foreign soil looking weak. I must be a strong man to give that national image that I am a leader of this country.' So, instead, I allowed two or three weeks to pass until I was fully stabilised, as I would leave only on the condition that I would be able to walk.

Just before my heart problem had first developed a very significant event had occurred: the death of my mother on 30 October 1974. She had been diagnosed with pancreatic cancer but she was not told too much detail about it – it was better that she was not exposed to unnecessary worry. No one knew much about that particular type of cancer, although we did know it was untreatable. Instead of concerning her about the sickness, which might have destroyed the remaining part of her life, we kept it as soft as possible. She went to Sydney to stay with my father and stepmother and then to Brisbane and the Gold Coast where she spent time playing with the birds and parrots at Currumbin. After her trip to Australia and about one month before she died, she decided to come and stay with me in Rabaul.

The doctor had already let us know that she was going to die soon. She was lying down in my house and I had to return to Port Moresby for a Cabinet meeting. I remember so clearly the last words she spoke to me before I left. I had said casually, 'I am off now.' I was trying to be a bit tough, to play down the situation so that she did not feel any fear. In that moment, though, she gave a bit of herself to me. She did not try and cuddle me or hold me back, she just responded quietly in Pidgin, *'Yu mas go nau, yu gat wok.'* ('You must go now, you've got work.') I did not want to leave. I really had a problem leaving her at that particular time. All the other times I would just say, 'See you, I am off,' and go. But this time I knew it was different. Even so, I obeyed her and two days later she died – in her sleep and peacefully.

My mother's last words left a big impression on me – in fact they are the most important and strongest words from her I can remember. She was always a very passionate person but she was incredibly brave at that particular moment. That last exchange, when I walked away from my dying mother to serve my country, made me the kind of politician I am today. She did not just let me go, in her generosity of spirit she reminded me that I had a duty to perform and I did it because she told me to. It was a message that gave me enormous strength and it was the making of my political character.

I do not know how to explain it but I have a very special place for my mother. How does one describe love? I am still very attached to her and in every place I live I have her photograph. We were always very respectful of my father and gave him the honour he deserved, but with my mother it was completely different. I used to fly a lot in small aircraft and there were times when it would be very dangerous if the plane got caught in the mountain clouds. I used to get quite frightened and the first person I thought of to get me out of the situation was my mother. I would talk to her and pray to her and then suddenly the clouds would lift and we would land safely. I would do the same thing if I was at sea and it began to get stormy. It may be superstitious but I have a supernatural kind of relationship with my mother and I believe she is still around.

My mother was buried in the Chinese section of the Rabaul cemetery, instead of in her village, because she was really a permanent migrant. She had made a lot of friends in the town and was well known there. It was the right thing to do and nobody ever questioned it. The distance between Nokon and Rabaul is not too great but back then communication was poor and travelling was not easy, so she was more or less cut off from her original family. Her headstone reads: 'In loving memory of my dear wife and our dearest mother, Miriam Tinkoris Chin. Died 30th October 1974 aged 65 years. Treasure her O Lord in your Eden of rest.'

Many years after the volcanic eruptions had largely ruined the cemetery, the Chinese community contributed about K100,000 to have all the ash removed from the graveyard so the graves could be exposed. Every year, on Mother's Day and the anniversary of her death, my brother Michael ensures that the boys in our family go and clean around her grave. We buy the best flowers we can get in Rabaul so her grave can be beautified.

After she died, I visited her grave with my father. As we stood there, he could sense that I was holding on to her and still grieving.

'Son,' he said, 'you can cry, you can feel very down. Your mother knows that you are a good boy and there is no amount of sympathy that will turn her back to life.'

This made me feel much stronger. I know that however much we grieve, we can never change what has already happened. Death is part of life and you do not jump into the grave with even the closest of your friends.

Chapter 10

How can you have dreams of something you've never seen before?

As we moved towards independence I was among a group of senior Papua New Guinean politicians who visited Australia to observe how their parliamentary system worked. In those days, everything was very orderly, very dignified, and I accepted that the Westminster system was the way for us to move forward. It's important to understand that we had only the white people's way of thinking and living – if they said a scent smelled good, we believed it. As the Westminster system was part of our inheritance from Australia why would we dare to say anything against it? I didn't. The decision for us to become part of the Commonwealth was also just a natural flow of events because we were part of the Australian family, and now we would become part of a community of nations who practised the same system of parliament.

We were due to meet with Australian Prime Minister Gough Whitlam but he ended up keeping us waiting for more than an hour. Albert Maori Kiki, who was quite an independent, vocal character and our Foreign Minister, started thumping the table and saying, 'Come on, we're going for self-government. I do not want to be treated this way.' He planned to walk out and I was just dragged along by him. I did not know why we were having this fight – I was just interested in the amount of money we would receive for self-government.

Fortunately, Somare stepped in and Maori Kiki was stopped at the door. We were persuaded to stay and allow Whitlam time to finish reading his brief and come to the meeting. The Premier of Queensland, Joh Bjelke-Petersen, was also invited along because we shared the common sea of the Torres Strait, and so there was some debate between us about equity in the distribution of fishing licences. He was a fair dinkum talker and knew exactly what he wanted. Even so, he had been the Premier for many years and had still not been to Papua New Guinea.

The meeting felt like a talk for the big boys, as I recall the level of discussion, with Whitlam talking above us. He came across as a political academic. It was clear he was well educated and a very learned man, and after he left office he became the Australian Ambassador to the United Nations Educational, Scientific and Cultural Organization (UNESCO). He would have had no trouble dealing with all the international issues because he was a man of history and culture. However, in my dealings with him, I felt he was not the type of man who would have a conversation because he might hear something that he could learn from, he would only be talking to convey his thoughts about the way things should be done.

I remember watching Whitlam after he had been on camera. He rushed up to us, cleaning his face, saying, 'It's melting!' Make-up was coming off his face. I did not understand it because we did not use make-up in Papua New Guinea. It seemed very artificial to me. Later on, when I became Prime

Minister, I started to think, 'I do not have the kind of make-up Whitlam had. I should.' It did come to my mind that it was part of the show, part of being Prime Minister, but I never got around to using it.

A few months later the Australian government changed and Malcolm Fraser became the Prime Minister and I found him to be a different person to deal with. Fraser did not talk as much and he had a habit of turning his head upwards so it appeared he would be looking down on others. Fraser was a well-informed person – equivalent to Whitlam – but it was clear they came from completely dissimilar backgrounds.

Fraser was, in Papua New Guinean terms, a Big Man, and a tall man. In spite of his imposing height, he was soft at heart and very sympathetic, much more compassionate concerning the needs of developing countries and more pragmatic in relationships. Although Australia was a relatively small player during this time in international affairs, it expressed views that affected all Commonwealth countries, not just the developed but also the developing ones. I found Fraser's manner to be quite aloof but his heart was genuine.

While all our government institutions were preparing for independence, it is important to mention the very significant and influential role the churches had already performed for many years – and continue to do so – in terms of the delivery of services. They were very progressive in providing schools and health services to the people. Churches of all denominations were an important part of the political process as well – if you did not have their support you were gone. They were really respected and revered and anybody who wore robes was extremely powerful. For example, the Catholic Bishop of Vunapope in Rabaul would be considered almost equivalent to the Pope.

Our Independence Day celebrations were massive and probably organised on a scale far superior to any other form of gathering in the country before or since. If you ask anybody why 16 September 1975 was chosen as the official date, I do not think they could tell you. Perhaps it was nominated because it was convenient for the Australian Governor-General Sir John Kerr or for Prince Charles, who came as the Queen's special representative. Gough Whitlam as Prime Minister of Australia came, as well as Malcolm Fraser, who was then Opposition leader. As Minister for Finance I was asked to look after all the international banking and finance visitors who were staying with the other dignitaries at a hotel overlooking Ela Beach. I was on hand to make sure everything ran smoothly; I had to smile a lot.

On the eve of Independence I was alerted very late at night that Imelda Marcos, the wife of the President of the Philippines, had arrived unexpectedly on a private aircraft with an entourage of about 30 people. I had personally met her husband, President Ferdinand Marcos, in 1972 as a result of a regional meeting at the Asian Development Bank in Manila. The Philippines was one of the top countries in Asia at that time, having been independent since 1946. It was strategically very important in terms of world power because of its relationship with the United States during the war and, as we were an emerging nation in the region, the Philippines wanted to be a good partner to us. Marcos facilitated all sorts of regional meetings and even, at my request, sent us a team of Filipino doctors, who eventually became a very important part of the medical network in rural Papua New Guinea.

I think it was because of this relationship that Imelda made the last-minute decision to come to our Independence Day celebrations. Imelda's group was hastily accommodated somewhere in the city and fortunately someone was there to receive her. Included in her entourage was something I had not really seen before: a team of about five or six personal beauty assistants. I do not know what people expected at Independence – a fully air-conditioned stadium perhaps – but instead we were all sitting in the stands of the open-air Hubert Murray Stadium on a really hot day, and I had to sit on a bench behind Imelda Marcos. I could not help but notice that as it got hotter she started to sweat and make-up began to run down her back. It appeared she was undergoing some kind of heat torture.

The Royal Papua New Guinea Constabulary performed at the event, as did a number of traditional dancers. It was an incredible spectacle. I do remember very clearly the Australian flag being lowered, folded and presented by John Guise to the Australian Governor-General Sir John Kerr. That was probably the most memorable moment for me.

Australia had governed a nation of two and a half million people spread across an enormous, rugged land, and they had done a good job. I believe what they did was quite appropriate for a country at that stage of development. Any other colonial power such as Britain or Germany would have run PNG in a completely different way. Australia was a very young country as they had only come into a Federation in 1901 and they were not entrenched in colonial rule – they themselves were treading on new ground. Australia had never decentralised a country before and neither had we, and I think because of that they were respectful, sensitive and cautious. Some say they could have done more but some of our people were only just coming out of the Stone Age. If Australia had brought in development too quickly, who would have appreciated it? Nobody.

A lot of Australians who had lived here before self-government stayed on. Most of the notable people could have reaped the benefits of the financial handshakes their government was offering once they returned home, but many of them had been in Papua New Guinea for years and did not want to leave. Even though they went through bouts of malaria and dysentery, their lives would have been exciting and many of them remained committed to our country for a long time to come.

Chapter 11

Our motto was to have a strong, stable and progressive government.

Shortly after Independence the political landscape in Australia underwent a dramatic change, brought on by the constitutional crisis of 11 November 1975, when Governor-General Sir John Kerr dismissed Prime Minister Gough Whitlam and then appointed Malcolm Fraser as caretaker Prime Minister. Andrew Peacock then became that country's Minister for Foreign Affairs. The budgetary situation at the time in Australia was very bad because of the 1973 international oil crisis. The country was in an economic downturn, inflation was high and unemployment was rising. During our colonial years there had been very little real negotiation between the two countries about the amount of money to be given to Papua New Guinea, but soon after Independence we had to go to Australia to negotiate our first budget.

Before that meeting I had gone to a banking conference in Melbourne and met with Andrew Peacock. I really liked him – he was very flamboyant with long hair. He would come in and grab my hand and talk my language, he was down to earth and friendly and because he was the same age as me we were really on the same level. At the conference we met by accident in the toilets of the hotel – he was down one end and I was at the other.

'Julius!' he yelled out. 'You have to give me the right figure. You have to ring me and do not ask for too much. Just give me exactly what you want.'

'Andrew,' I said, 'I do not want fat. Fat would be very unhealthy for a new country. I am not going to ask you for more than what's necessary.' I was aiming for a budget that would just contain the country's flow towards self-reliance. I was worried that having too much money might mean we would start to have problems with fingers in the pot.

'Well,' he replied, 'this is my telephone number – you just ring me.'

We went into Independence with over 75 per cent of our budget being from Australian aid, so those were the parameters I had to work towards. The advice I had was that $125 million would be able to carry us through, so that was the figure I stuck with. Michael Somare then met with Fraser in a private meeting and I got a phone call from one of our senior public servants, who is currently our High Commissioner to Australia, Charles Lepani, saying, 'We can open up the champagne now. We got exactly what you asked for.' Apparently there had been a big fight between Peacock, Fraser and the Treasurer Phillip Lynch over the amount, but in the end we had our post-Independence budget.

After Independence, I tied the kina to a fixed basket of currencies – these were the countries we traded with the most. We were not ready to float our currency internationally. I used to get a call on a Sunday from Lynch to let me know of any currency movements relating to the Australian dollar because any change would impact us. Lynch would ring me at twelve o'clock to tell me that the Australian dollar had devalued or revalued. There was no business being transacted on a Sunday so there could not be any suggestion of impropriety in him giving me this information.

The Australians went through a big depreciation between 1975 and 1979 – by about 17.5 per cent at one point – so we also went through a very hectic period. I was glad that Papua New Guinea had its own currency at this time, otherwise we would have really suffered. I was enormously sensitive to this because I had made a national commitment to a project that was controlled internationally. I made sure I had very good people working in Papua New Guinea who were in touch with the Treasury of Australia so we knew the likely range of depreciation. I would then set the kina on the parity that I wanted. If they went down 17.5, I only went down 12.5 per cent. I maintained a 5 per cent advantage, which was the right thing to do so the kina would remain as strong as possible.

After the elections of 1977 the United Party, led by Tei Abal, came up with pretty good numbers. They had over 30 members while Somare's Pangu Party had around 25 members. Our People's Progress Party (PPP) had 18 to 22 members, so with either party we could have made a very good majority. We were approached by both the United Party and the Pangu Party to do so. Somare came all the way to Rabaul to plead his case with me to form a government with them. Tei Abal, who was in Port Moresby, contacted Harry Hoeler, the brother of my brother's wife, Maria Hoeler, to ask me to join with them.

As a party we could have taken the prime ministership, but I felt that two years of Independence was too short a period, that a change might be destabilising. We needed time, more maturity,

I had a carefree childhood. Here I'm in our garden in Rabaul, aged nine or ten.

I was very close to my sister Amelia, even though she was eight years older.

After the war, we moved in with Uncle Chin Him (back row, second from right) and his family in Rabaul. My father, Chin Pak, is to the right of his brother and I'm in the front row, fourth from the left. I was about six or seven years old.

With Joe Chan (middle) and friend Gerard Tam (right) at Marist College Ashgrove, c. 1955. I always liked wearing that blazer.

After college in Australia, I worked as an audit clerk. This was taken in Maupa village, Central Province.

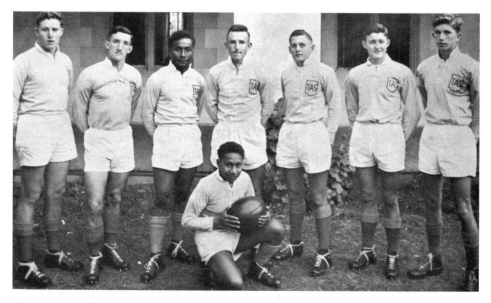

The Associated Schools' rugby team, 1956. I remember all those boys. I'm kneeling at the front and Joe is standing behind me. Image courtesy of Marist College Ashgrove.

Stella and I on our wedding day with my mother, father and stepmother (seated left to right), and extended family and friends, including my half-brother, Bosco (far right).

Stella in 1976 with our children (left to right): Vanessa, Mark, baby Toea and Byron.

First predominantly Papua New Guinean government formed in 1972 under Chief Minister Michael Somare (left to right): Thomas Kavali, me, Reuben Taureka, John Poe, Bruce Jephcott, Michael Somare, Paulus Arek, Paul Lapun, Gavera Rea, Boyamo Sali, Ebia Olewale, Albert Maori Kiki, Donatus Mola, John Guise, Kaibelt Diria, Moses Sasakila, Iambakey Okuk.

Image courtesy of Denis Williams and the *PNG Post-Courier*.

Young leaders: I'm with Michael Somare (left) and John Guise (right). Image courtesy of *Pangu Pati Nius* 1972, National Library of Australia, MFM PMB DOC 465.

To my mother, with love [signature] 1973.

My first political portrait, taken in New York in 1973, and dedicated to my mother, Miriam Tinkoris (inset). She died of cancer the following year.

The 'financial brains' of PNG's banking system: me, Henry ToRobert,
Ross Garnaut and Mekere Morauta before Independence.

Prince Charles at the Independence Day ceremony, Port Moresby, 16 September 1975.
Image courtesy of Denis Williams and the *PNG Post-Courier*.

Soon after I became Prime Minister in 1980, a civil crisis erupted in New Hebrides (Vanuatu), so I deployed troops to help quell the unrest.

Somare condemned the purchase of the Grumman Gulfstream II aircraft, *The Kumul*, but many officials used it to travel throughout the South Pacific.

Left: Andrew Peacock and I had a great working relationship. In 1981 we opened the PNG High Commission in Canberra. Image courtesy of the National Archives of Australia, A6180, 9/1/81/15.

Below: I live in two worlds: my political one and my traditional one. I was brought up between cultures so it is natural and easy for me to adjust. Here I'm participating in a special ceremony for my 70th birthday.

a longer period of consolidation. That's why I got my team to support Somare. I caved in for the sake of stability and because of the PPP's commitment to a strong government. Due to the strength of our numbers, though, we secured prominent ministries, like Transport and Works, Trade and Finance. Somare gave us these because we were running them very well at Independence and, of course, he had to form a government.

I had run a very tight ship since before Independence and the PPP worked well as a team. We were highly disciplined, constructive and creative in policymaking. We came forward with a lot of significant legislation; all our guns were firing. The early years of Independence was the period when institutions like the National Broadcasting Corporation (NBC) and Air Niugini, which had been established during self-government, were very successful. Warren Dutton, a member of the PPP and Minister for Police, was also the leader of Government Business in the House and he came forward with a lot of significant legislation. Bruce Jephcott was our Minister for Transport, and so we had major roads being constructed, and we were also negotiating with the International Monetary Fund (IMF), the World Bank and the Asian Development Bank.

In 1977 I was removed – with my agreement – as Minister for Finance and appointed as Minister for Primary Industries, remaining as Deputy Prime Minister. I was replaced by Barry Holloway, who was someone I really respected – in terms of seasoned politicians he was much more mature than I was at the time, having been a Kiap for many years. I was happy about the change – it was time I moved on and the portfolio I took on was a very attractive one. I had control of forestry, fisheries, livestock and agriculture, which was great as these industries formed the backbone of the PNG economy.

One enterprise I supported was Ramu Sugar. At that time all the sugar we were consuming was imported from the Colonial Sugar Refining Company (CSR) in Australia. Somare consulted Charles Lepani and David Beatty from Canada, an economic advisor, who recommended against Papua New Guinea going into sugar production. It was argued that the import figures were so low that it was not worth us going into competition with CSR because the arrangement was pretty good. I still went down to see CSR and find out whether they would feel uneasy about us going into sugar production. At that time, Papua New Guinea was just a little peanut consumer of sugar – a lot of our people could not even afford to buy a packet of rice let alone sugar. The chairman of CSR told me that the company would not feel any impact if Papua New Guinea went it alone – they were fine. After I presented my proposal, Somare's advisors felt it was not viable and the idea was dropped. I took it up again when I became Prime Minister in 1980 and today Ramu Agri Industries produces on average 34,000 tonnes of sugar per year and employs 4000 people in the sugar, beef and oil palm enterprises of the business.

During this time I initiated many other policies relating to tuna, fisheries, forestry and crops. Every oil palm plantation in the country was supported by me, including those at Kimbe, Oro and Milne Bay. I also developed fisheries policies and the Forestry College at Wau–Bulolo.

As a party the PPP projected policy ideas into every area of government. We even developed the Gavien rubber resettlement scheme near Angoram in East Sepik Province, which was right in Somare's electoral heartland. The so-called Gang of Four – Charles Lepani, Rabbie Namaliu, Anthony Siaguru and Mekere Morauta – were advisors to Michael Somare. I believe they had already begun to assess the political situation and were worried about the high-performing role of the PPP. Looking ahead, they were probably concerned about the outcome of the next elections.

About six months after the 1977 elections, Somare began to make decisions without consulting us. Initially we were okay about it, and we followed the principle of the convention that he was the leader and it was within his realm of authority. However, it was not long before we felt he was going too far. He started splitting ministries to dilute the PPP's influence, including my ministry. We decided if he did not correct it then we would have to leave the government.

In 1978 Somare had been in Wewak and I think his advisors, the Gang of Four, had flown there to outline the political situation and persuade him to split even more portfolios. I am not quite sure when he signed these instruments of change but I do not think he was in his right mind when he did so. The Pangu Party was all over the place at this time – the only thing they had done was establish the National Investment and Development Authority, but they really did not know what else to do. They even talked about stopping foreign investment in the country.

When we found out about these changes it was a definite breach of our original Memorandum of Understanding signed on the formation of the second government, which was to have meaningful consultations and that the allocation of ministries must be jointly agreed. We could not continue to pledge our support when we knew that any agreements we made could be changed at any time. In early November 1978, we decided we would resign en masse. It was an historical political decision made on a matter of principle, which is very rare.

'We made you the Prime Minister of this country,' I told him. 'You have breached our agreement and that is something I am not prepared to allow my party to be subjected to. If we are going to be strong we have to live up to the leadership agreement. You failed, so we will leave you.' When I told Somare, he had tears rolling down his face. He was very stressed during the meeting and was actually pleading for us to stay with him in government. He said he would reconsider and appeared to genuinely feel he may have made the wrong decision.

Iambakey Okuk was now leading the National Party and they were standing by in Opposition. We could have formed a new government with them but we were not thinking about seeking power or forming another government, far from it. However, even as he was speaking to me, Somare was ten miles ahead of us. While he was talking as if in grief, with tears running down his face and pleading with us to stay – this was probably the *sana* (chiefly) part of him – his team was behind the scenes in another office holding a meeting with Raphael Doa, now a significant voice in the United Party. We had been naive. We did not understand then that politics in Papua New Guinea did not necessarily play by the rules. The Pangu Party already had a strategy to form government with the United Party, so that when we moved out they would move in, and that is exactly what happened.

The questions of power and monetary influence were of much less significance in government at that time as there were fewer opportunities for politicians to become involved in dealings with foreign companies looking to gain a foothold in the country. If it was today, with all the multimillion-kina projects to be considered, the government would be formed through a completely different process, and politicians with possible access to private funds would be more influential. My relationship with Somare had generally been a very good one in the early days of Independence – we called each other Michael and Julius. Later it became Mr Somare and Mr Chan. In a typical Melanesian way, however, politics never really became a long-term barrier to our friendship. He may have distrusted me, and I probably felt the same about him, but when it came to other areas of life we were friends. In those initial years we were going in the same direction – we had both made promises to the people and we remained committed to those deeply personal obligations. We were also aware of what was happening in other countries that had gained independence, with chaos following soon afterwards, particularly in Africa – fortunately the PNG temperament was somewhat different from the mindset in African countries.

The PPP left the government and became the minority party on the crossbenches, which meant we could either support or oppose the government on principle. Okuk remained the Opposition leader and leader of the National Party, and he had some very strong members on his team. We remained a minority party for two years, which was difficult because we were quite restricted in our ability to criticise some of the policies we had helped to create – even if we had not totally agreed with the policy when we were in government. We generally took the middle line – supporting the government some times and at others supporting the Opposition.

Even though we were not in government, the members of the PPP continued to work together as co-operatively as we had before. We still had a lot to say about inflation, the annual budget and matters like the Electoral Development Fund, which was originally devised in the early 1980s to fast-track specific development projects and deliver services. We believed that some of the basic services could be delivered more quickly if the local member used the funds to work together with their local councils. The fund began with about K5000 and then increased to K50,000, and by 2016 this amount could be as much as K15 million a year under the District Services Improvement Program (DSIP). The DSIP, however, has come under sustained criticism for many years, with concerns over how these funds have been spent. The majority of leaders charged for misconduct in office have been accused of the misappropriation of electoral development funds and quite a number of them have been dismissed from office.

The DSIP does build up the capacity of the members of parliament, particularly those in open seats, to have sufficient funds to go to the elections, to buy votes, to actually influence the voting patterns. But that was never the purpose of the funds and this money has ended up being used at the members' discretion – making it open game for misappropriation.

Without us Somare carried on, but not with the lustre of the combination we'd had before. He had made a political marriage of convenience with the United Party, a party that had been in limbo for a long time. They were talking in two different languages and were often at loggerheads with one another. The United Party had come into office for the sake of convenience and they took over not knowing the course that had been charted.

There were several issues that plagued the last two years of the Somare government and one was the Nahau Rooney case in 1979. Rooney, who had been the Minister for Justice, had publicly criticised the Supreme Court for overruling a Cabinet decision on a deportation order and was jailed for contempt of court. It was a major event and was all over the papers. As soon as she went to jail – she spent only a day there – Somare's Cabinet used their power of mercy to let her out. This decision caused a mass resignation of all the expatriate judges and hundreds of prisoners broke out of the jails. There was a huge outcry as people were very concerned about the precedent being set – Rooney had tried to rein in the court, an independent arm of the government, and now Somare had compromised himself by allowing her out of jail. She was a member of the Pangu Party and was close to Somare but there were more connotations than that. She was the only woman minister and she had tried to tamper with the court's independent decision – that was totally unacceptable to me, because parliament must honour the Constitution.

At the same time there were divisions between the disciplinary forces and the police, the economy was not running well, inflation was high, there were issues with the currency exchange rate and there was a growing budget deficit. When I was Finance Minister my staff had close links with the Australian Treasury and were well informed. Now Papua New Guinea was not really acting fast enough to make its currency adjustments on time. The connection between the two countries had declined since I had left the Ministry of Finance and this had left the economy at a disadvantage.

By 1979 the image of the government was somewhat tarnished. People were losing confidence and feeling the pinch of tougher economic times – there was uncertainty over the value of the kina, the operations of the Finance Department, the levels of foreign reserves and inflation. The growing political sentiment was that Somare could no longer be trusted – there was diminishing confidence in his leadership and the Pangu Party was involved in businesses that were being questioned.

Somare had the numbers but no policy guidelines, no real implementation machinery. It was Okuk, really, as the Opposition leader, who calculated that we could no longer allow this government to continue. The time was right for a change.

CHAPTER 12

Why did I need to solve it? Now that I am able to reminisce I realise there were simply some things I did because I was the right man at that time to make it happen.

By early 1980 Vanessa was old enough to go to boarding school and we chose to send her to Lourdes Hill in Hawthorne, Brisbane, run by the Sisters of the Good Samaritan. When Stella and I went to drop her off at the school, I found it very difficult to say goodbye. When it came time to go I cried openly – I felt so heavy in my heart about leaving her. I had always felt very close to Vanessa even though my work had robbed me of so much time with her. This parting marked the end of an era. Although she cried too, Vanessa was strong and so was Stella, far stronger than me. I just felt overwhelmed, as though I had lost my pearl.

Vanessa was happy at that school. However, because she had been brought up in Rabaul, it was not so easy for her to excel in the same way as other Australian-educated kids and she had to work hard to catch up. I arrived back in Port Moresby after settling Vanessa into school and was met at the airport by Iambakey Okuk and his team. Okuk had been calculating his position, and he told me that we should not allow things to rot any further, that we should retrieve the state of the nation and insisted that we should form an alternative government.

'We're taking over and we want to put you up as the Prime Minister,' he said.

I did not commit immediately but his words played on my mind and inculcated into my thinking. It was not long before I decided that we were going to challenge Michael Somare.

The Constitution made the process of changing government very clear and, even though there were some objections against the motion, these were resolved. There was no question of whether the standing orders were in line; the Constitution stated there had to be seven days' notice and we could change the government. This vote, the first ever made in the PNG National Parliament, resulted in a 57 to 49 vote against Somare.

After the Nahau Rooney case I do not think Somare wanted any more trouble so he followed the Constitution, accepted defeat, and I became Prime Minister on 11 March 1980. The handover went very smoothly. The police knew exactly what to do, the government acknowledged the defeat, the game changed and Governor-General Tore Lokoloko accepted us as government at a swearing-in ceremony.

The main priority when I became Prime Minister was to address the country's quite serious economic problems. My attitude was: 'We have to fix it and fix it now.' Our people felt the economic burden and the increasing cost of goods because of international inflation issues and poor internal policies. Somare had not been kicked out just because we had the numbers, but because there had been a lot of unco-ordinated decisions made for short-term political reasons – a lot of guns had been pointing at him before he left office.

Okuk was an unpredictable character – too radical to have captured the numbers to become Prime Minister on his own. I appointed him the Deputy Prime Minister and Minister for Civil Aviation. The Melanesian Alliance, which included John Kaputin and John Momis, also supported our government. With them it was quite a good coalition of people who had played a significant role at Independence. John Kaputin, whom I appointed as the Minister for Finance, was a very strong character, highly political, with a fixed mind – he got on well with people who could talk his language and was able to adjust himself to different levels of discussion. He was not particularly innovative or hard-working but he had good people around him. Working with Okuk, however, was like working with a time bomb. I would have called him 'a man of action, followed by delayed reasoning', largely because he had many ideas that he wanted to see have an impact overnight.

I visited Chimbu and went to his home, Pari village, on top of the mountain. Chimbu was a very important economic centre with the biggest co-operative coffee movement. Okuk's people had planted crops on the other side of the mountain range, which meant that each morning they had a long arduous walk to their gardens or they would have to stay overnight in the bush. Doing that run every day or every second day was not an easy thing and the people who lived there were strong, pragmatic and courageous. It was – and still is – a tough environment and you have to be strong to survive. Seeing where he grew up influenced the way I assessed Okuk and I began to understand him more. He had a capacity for quick decision-making and one decision he made was very controversial.

As Minister for Civil Aviation Okuk travelled to Canada, with my permission, along with his chief advisor, Jeff Wall. While they were there he decided to enter into a lease agreement to buy four DHC-7 or Dash 7 aircraft – without any authority from Cabinet. He had thought it was a grand idea that the Dash 7 could land at remote airports, such as Kundiawa near where he came from. Wall drafted a statement announcing the deal.

Kaputin and Momis, who was appointed Minister for Decentralisation, saw themselves as guardians against corrupt practices and they were very angry about the deal. Momis, a former priest who was very serious in his delivery of speeches, was incredibly honest. Several other ministers, including Warren Dutton, who was the Minister for Police, were also angry because they believed Okuk had acted outside the rules. During Cabinet meetings it became highly emotional – people started pounding desks, throwing chairs and shouting – it almost got to the point where I thought there was going to be an actual fight. Even though they had stretched my patience, I maintained my cool.

'We have gone beyond political arguments. You people are about to reach a fighting point,' I told them. 'I will suspend the Cabinet and you can go outside. I will not allow the most important executive of this nation to be subjected to this sort of behaviour. Come back when you are ready.' I had to adjourn Cabinet several times to allow the ministers to finish their shouting matches and give them time to cool down.

At one point Okuk told me that he would pull out of the transaction.

'Look, I have had enough of this. Just forget it and cancel the deal,' he said. But having been to Chimbu and seen the background of his life, I refused his offer.

'Friend, it is not that easy,' I told him. 'You have made a decision, you've committed the government. If it was wrong then you will have to carry it and if it is right, then it is a victory for you. You cannot walk away.'

I called in the board of Air Niugini – Joe Tauvasa was the Managing Director at the time – and the Department of Civil Aviation joined us so we could establish who had the authority to buy the aircraft. It was then that we found out that Okuk had the authority – even he did not know it – to enter into the contract and all he had to do was get the directors of Air Niugini to approve it. Okuk had not been acting contrary to law in any form in making this decision.

The viability and performance of the Dash 7 aircraft – with short landing and short take-off – were established, and so the board agreed and the deal went ahead. It fulfilled Okuk's dreams that aircraft from the national carrier would be able to land in his remote province.

'You won the day, Iambakey,' I told him. 'You won the day.'

I had not been Prime Minister for very long when the secessionist crisis erupted in Vanuatu (then known as New Hebrides). The recently elected government, which was headed by Father Walter Lini and the Vanua'aku Pati, was preparing for the country's independence in July 1980. Vanuatu had been a condominium ruled by Britain and France for quite some years, which I imagine was quite a complicated arrangement. The islands had been colonised by both the British and French in the eighteenth century, shortly after Captain James Cook arrived, and the two powers later signed an agreement. In 1975 they created a joint administration of both local and European officials, and some powers were devolved to an elected assembly. However, as independence approached, there was an armed uprising against the plans and a bid for secession on Espiritu Santo Island, led by

Jimmy Stevens, a nationalist and politician. Stevens was the leader of what they called the Nagriamel movement, and he declared the independence of Espiritu Santo and apparently started to refer to himself as the Prime Minister.

The New Hebrides government asked Britain and France to send troops to put an end to the armed rebellion but France did not want the United Kingdom to deploy troops. The Prime Minister-elect, Walter Lini, began to look around for help closer to home. We had planned to attend the South Pacific Forum meeting in Kiribati. I was flying in on the government aircraft, so I asked the Commander of the PNG Defence Force (PNGDF), Ted Diro, to come with me and join the discussion. At midnight on the day we arrived, we met with Father Walter Lini and Barak Sope, his Chief of Staff, who later became the Prime Minister of Vanuatu. Father Lini said he had asked for help from other governments in the region – New Zealand Prime Minister Robert Muldoon and Australian Prime Minister Malcolm Fraser – who had refused. The reason was probably the potential cost and perhaps because they were white countries and they did not want to be seen as bullies or to upset the French or British government.

I sent Diro to find out the situation on the ground and give me his military advice. Back home and after a lot of Cabinet discussion and opposition, we made a commitment to despatch, for the first time, defence force troops outside of Papua New Guinea. We passed the *Defence Force (Deployment Abroad) Act*, which was then challenged in the courts by Michael Somare, now the leader of the Opposition, on the grounds that it was unconstitutional. This challenge was ultimately not upheld.

I have reflected since on why I agreed to send troops to Vanuatu. I thought that the metropolitan powers were happy enough to get together in the South Pacific Forum (now the Pacific Islands Forum) because it helped them to secure votes in the international arena of the United Nations. However, we had to be fair. Papua New Guinea was part of the forum and I felt we should support Vanuatu, that the friendship had to be translated into something real. I told my colleagues that we had to be genuine about things in life, that we should have ideals to live up to.

We had initially arranged for the PNGDF band to play at Vanuatu's Independence Day celebrations – now they were going to be accompanied by a special regiment, which underwent a month of intensive training. I asked Diro to give me a guarantee that no one would be shot, because if one of our men had been lost I probably would have been hung.

'My soldiers are ready,' he said. 'As for me guaranteeing that you will not lose a soldier, I cannot. All I can say to you is that we are the best jungle fighters in the southern hemisphere.'

Under our agreement with Father Lini, the PNGDF troops were operating under his control. I was confident that as we were being led by authority of the Prime Minister, acting in accordance with the new Constitution of Vanuatu, that he had the legal right to enforce this mandate. Soon after the PNGDF arrived in Vanuatu, they met the French Foreign Legion on Espiritu Santo.

Commander Tony Huai, guided by Diro, began to monitor the movements of rebel leader Jimmy Stevens. Diro had to report to me at six o'clock every evening. I would ask him, 'What happened today? What did you do today? And what are you doing tonight?' One morning Stevens went to have a wash, which was when our soldiers captured him. Not long after that, one of the rebels fired a shot during the night and in retaliation our soldier shot dead one of the attackers. The word quickly went around the country – the Papua New Guinean soldiers were practising *puri puri* (magic), because they could kill at night and when they fired a shot they never missed. The people in Vanuatu are Melanesians like us, so this was a very commonly held belief. Soon after, a grenade killed Stevens' son – again, action undertaken by our soldiers – when he did not stop at a roadblock, and not long after that the rebellion ended.

I was happy with the outcome. The troops stayed on in Vanuatu and the army band played at the Independence Day celebrations on 30 July. Following on from our successful military mission in what some of the media referred to as the 'Coconut War', I strongly believed that Vanuatu's situation should never be repeated and that there should be a regional peacekeeping force established to solve this kind of problem in Pacific countries. I put this submission before the South Pacific Forum but it was either deferred or put aside by Australia and New Zealand, probably for the same reasons they were reluctant to assist Vanuatu. The two countries were very powerful at the time and, although the other Pacific countries were in favour of my proposal, I had to leave it. Many years later the idea was taken up when the Regional Assistance Mission to the Solomon Islands (RAMSI) was established in 2003. Australia was assisted by New Zealand, Fiji and several other Pacific nations.

In 1980 I was given a KBE, a Knight Commander of the Most Excellent Order of the British Empire. I had already been awarded a CBE (Commander of the Order of the British Empire) in 1975 for the work I had done for PNG's currency, banks and financial institutions. Initially I did not want to go to Buckingham Palace to receive my knighthood as I thought I would have to wear a top hat and tails and I knew I would not feel comfortable. I loathe extremely formal occasions and I really just wanted to say *maski* (let it go). Of course this was not possible so I agreed to go to London. I just wanted the ordeal to be over as quickly as possible. However, after some inquiries were made, I was given a dispensation by the Palace to wear a simple suit.

Stella accompanied me on this trip. After the ceremony, where I had to kneel and was tapped on both shoulders with a sword, we all had a cup of tea together at Buckingham Palace. The room where we went was incredibly majestic and the Queen was very nice, and very well informed about Papua New Guinea. She had visited the country in her younger days, in the 1950s, and knew a great deal about it.

The following year I was made a member of the Privy Council, the body that advises the Queen and has acted as the higher court of appeal for the Commonwealth. During that time I helped to form the quorum on the council that made several final decisions, although what they were I cannot recall. Many years later, in 1994, I met the Queen again, when she made me a Grand Cross – the highest grade in knighthoods and the highest order given to ordinary citizens. This time I was not as worried about the ceremony as it was quite informal. The Queen presented me with a very special box of medals.

For a long time there had been increasing disquiet over the impact of the Panguna copper mine and related land issues. The mine had been established in the early 1970s by Bougainville Copper Limited, a subsidiary of the Australian company Conzinc Rio Tinto, after the discovery of about one billion tonnes of copper in the Crown Prince Range. The mine began production in 1972 after an agreement with the Papua New Guinean government, which was a 20 per cent shareholder – the mine contributed around 20 per cent of government revenue. Bougainvilleans received a very small share, less than half a per cent, of the total profit. Part of the original agreement was that the terms of the lease should be reviewed every five years.

Like New Ireland, the land on Bougainville was passed down through a matrilineal system. The people's attitude was that they had owned the land for thousands of years – in their worldview they owned everything, on top, under and in the water. By the time I had become Prime Minister the mine lease had not been reviewed, as it should have been. Leo Hannett was then the Premier of Bougainville and John Momis the Regional Member. They were pushing for a review of the package and this should have been looked at seriously.

I decided to take the Cabinet to the Bougainville capital, Arawa, to talk through the issue. Hannett came but Momis, who was a member of my Cabinet, arrived very late, sending a signal to me that he was not happy. The government should have had a clear position to present to the Bougainvilleans, but we were unable to agree on what that should be. Hannett, in the absence of Momis, was too timid to give us a guide so our government team was quite weak. I am not clear about what the Bougainvilleans thought, but the main points we put forward must have been unacceptable to them because our ideas were rejected.

I later went again to Arawa with Rabbie Namaliu, who later became Prime Minister from 1988 to 1992, to talk to the leaders but I could never really tell what was at the back of their minds. I thought we gave them a very reasonable offer, however, I did not feel we really got the co-operation of the Bougainvilleans. The people missed out and we had breached the conditions for a review, which was disappointing. I really wanted to resolve the issue before the upcoming election in 1982 but it did not happen. It was a wasted chance.

Chapter 13

I did not take on the role of Prime Minister to use the position for something else and enjoy it; I am not very good at socialising. I did it because it was a job that needed to be done.

Becoming Prime Minister was quite a natural role for me because of my previous experiences in managing a business and as Minister for Finance. In a sense I had already been groomed for the job. One of the values I prized very highly was that the members of my Cabinet would be self-disciplined and punctual. If people were late for a meeting I would lock them out of the room until it was time for a recess. I remember Noel Levi, the Foreign Affairs and Trade Minister, was late a couple of times because the power had gone out and the lifts were not working. Levi carried a little bit of extra weight and had to climb nine floors to get to the meeting. Unfortunately for him, I locked him out until we stopped for a break.

I was organised and I had priorities on who I would see. I made it clear that business houses or corporate people must give me sufficient notice. But the fellow on the street who had no telephone but was someone I was representing needed no advance warning – if they wanted to see me and I had time, then I would see them first. After that I would see my ministers, then the departments and my staff together. On the days parliament was sitting, I would program a schedule of meetings throughout the day so that everyone knew what to do during debates and what to vote on legislation.

I took on this job demanding efficiency in the public service and productivity. My style of leadership was to be open to consultation but also to be an independent decision-maker. It was my idea to start a more selective engagement policy with other countries rather than the 'friends to all and enemies to none' policy that Michael Somare carried through at Independence. Sometimes we don't choose our friends, and nor do we choose our enemies.

As far as Australia was concerned, however, their paternalistic attitude remained. If Australians wanted to visit Papua New Guinea, they did not always give us sufficient warning – many years later this was still the case with Foreign Affairs Minister Alexander Downer. I always preferred to give prior approval to anyone visiting except for the Prime Minister of another country – not because of pride but just simply because I wanted to offer respect to the head of another nation.

There were many challenges during my prime ministership. John Kaputin had to spend a lot of time with the Governor of the Central Bank and me to determine our course of action. The World Bank was imposing conditions on countries because of the international economic crisis. Over that period we gradually brought the economy back into shape and a budget that was reasonably balanced.

One of the most controversial decisions my government made was to spend K5 million on a Grumman Gulfstream II aircraft. It was named *The Kumul*, after the PNG bird of paradise. I had realised over the years that we were disadvantaged by not having access to an aircraft that could take leaders to routes not covered by Air Niugini or Qantas. This was particularly true when it came to travelling around all the tiny atolls of the Pacific – something that was becoming increasingly important if we wanted to establish stronger relationships with the other smaller island states.

Somare, as Opposition leader, condemned the purchase and continually used the issue against me right up until the 1982 elections. Somare, of course, had been a reporter and he knew how to use the media far better than I did. He was able to drum up all these sentiments against the purchase and many people thought that I had pinched their money to buy the aircraft for myself. His message was: 'You are wasteful, you are indulgent and this is inappropriate for a country of this size.' However, *The Kumul* was used very heavily and not just by me or my Cabinet; it was also used by Governor-General Sir Tore Lokoloko and Chief Justice Sir Buri Kidu. In 1981 I used the aircraft to attend the Commonwealth Heads of Government Meeting in Melbourne. One of the most memorable moments in my prime ministerial life was when the captain called the control tower in Canberra.

'This is *Kumul One*. We are ready for take-off.' In that moment I felt terrific, that we were really, truly independent. It was a most satisfying experience during my prime ministership, a very special memory.

I was also very fortunate that the prime ministership allowed me to meet some very impressive people, particularly other world leaders at the time, such as British Prime Minister Margaret Thatcher, Indian Prime Minister Indira Gandhi, and Lee Kuan Yew, the Prime Minister of Singapore. Lee liked to talk about how the city-state had gained independence from Malaysia and he always became very repetitive in telling how he organised the transformation of Singapore. During the 1981 Commonwealth Heads of Government Meeting in Melbourne, Lee would be talking, Thatcher would be throwing critical ideas forward and Australian Prime Minister Malcolm Fraser would be responding with all the statistics at his fingertips. They were among the best international leaders who commanded major democracies, and were able to argue the points of policy that were relevant to their parts of the world. I was deeply impressed by them. Thatcher had immense experience of being a colonialist and she would contribute a lot of information about other former colonies in Africa, for example, which were joining the Commonwealth. I would sit among these leaders, listening very intently to their arguments and points. I was fascinated. I admired their capacity, their knowledge and their delivery of ideas.

My salary as Prime Minister was K12,500 but, while I could have happily lived on that, I had children to educate. Like my father, I had to find a way to pay for them. Up until this point I had owned 30 per cent of our family business, Coastal Shipping, and over the years we had built up a substantial business with eleven ships. My younger brother, Michael, was running the company and we had almost knocked our rival Steamships out of all the routes because we were so efficient and had a more personalised service. We made sure we ran on time – the boats would leave Rabaul and arrive at five o'clock in the morning at the Lutheran Shipping Wharf in Lae, discharge the cargo and load up again, with the boat leaving at 5 p.m. for Rabaul. I was hoping that the company could distribute more dividends to supplement my income but it was on a course of expansion, and so I suggested they buy me out. I sold my shares and used some of that money to buy a house at Macgregor, a southern suburb of Brisbane, so that we could have a family home in Australia for the kids. I was very fortunate in that purchase because the kina was very strong against the Australian dollar at the time.

Vanessa had been the first of my children to go to school overseas and then I started to send the boys. They all attended primary school in Rabaul but I chose to send them to Australia for high school because there were not many choices in Papua New Guinea at the time. There was a high school in Rabaul but it was pretty disorganised. They would have had to go either to Port Moresby or senior high at Keravat or Sogeri. If they'd gone to any of these schools, they would have had to board, and so they would have been away from home anyway. To be able to send the kids to Australia was something we all worked hard towards. Having said that, it took a while to get used to the idea. I had always lived among family – when I was young I lived with two families. I thought that was supposed to be life – to have a family, to have kids and extended family close by. Producing children and allowing adoption between family members has always been very common in Papua New Guinea and quite an ordinary, normal thing to do.

All of the boys went to Marist College Ashgrove because I felt a loyalty to the school and because I had a strong sense of connection to the place. One important aspect for me was the discipline. They were definitely much stricter than the state schools. During my time, the brothers were very harsh; however, by the time my boys went there, corporal punishment had waned. I also thought it would be easier to get them into Ashgrove because there might have been obstacles getting them into other colleges overseas without any previous background connection. Even now, if my grandson or my brother's grandson wanted to go to Ashgrove and I made a recommendation, the college would automatically consider it. It is one of those traditions.

Some of the staff who taught me were still at the school and were very good. There was one teacher, Brother Frank McMahon or

Brother Francis, who was the senior football coach of the First XV, who later went to the Solomon Islands and taught at Gizo in the Western Province. As Prime Minister I visited the Solomons and the first thing I asked for was to see Brother Francis. They flew him in and he joined me for lunch.

Byron got into trouble at school because he was not academically inclined – he was born differently in his personality, his emotions and his kindness. There was radiance in his way of life. He was very strong; he studied karate and could crack bricks. He liked to join up with some of his classmates and they would jump the fence at night to go to midnight dances in Fortitude Valley. He was caught and given a warning, but then he was caught again. Fortunately I had an old school friend, Bernie Knapp, who lived near Ashgrove and was friendly with the principal. With his help, I just approached the situation respectfully, intelligently, dealt with it, and then went back to Port Moresby. The fellow who did most of the talking was Bernie. He was the right man to deal with the matter because he was a lawyer and he could speak in the kind of language he might use in court to defend a client. In the end Byron was only suspended for two weeks. After that he went back to school and finished his senior years.

Vanessa is the child who is most like me and is the one closest to me. She is very firm on things and clear on what she wants to do. She is a determined person and able to depend on herself to get things done. Vanessa has been able to strike up friendships with people who can work with her and listen to her. Although she's a woman, she now has all sorts of men working under her, which is something that still does not occur too frequently in any culture.

My style of parenting was probably the same type of discipline I used to govern the nation – I would have borrowed a lot of that temperament from my father. I thought I was quite firm in telling them what they could and could not do and, generally speaking, they were reasonable kids. I thought Byron was too soft, Mark could be too rigid, and Toea was just happy-go-lucky. In them I had a mix of everything. But the kids always knew what I was like and what I expected. They learned from the way I demanded things and the way I commanded the people around me in business. They grasped a lot from those experiences and they just seemed to fall into line. It was not something extraordinary I had to do. When they were teenagers I do not think the boys were drinking or womanising, and if they were smoking they kept it to themselves.

I had come into government to repair the failings of the Somare government, and I had to carry all their sins. We went to the 1982 election as a government that had kept the country going in very difficult times. I knew it was not going to be easy. The issue of the Grumman aircraft was repeatedly fuelled by Somare, along with the controversial decision by Iambakey Okuk to buy the Dash 7s from Canada. Those two things became major election issues. Papua New Guineans have short memories. They just look at the man in the chair and say, 'He is the problem.'

It was not my style to go to the elections by bashing the Opposition – I focussed on providing confident policies for the people. Somare, who was a political strategist, got his message across very effectively – he just hammered the issue of the jet to get rid of me. He kept on saying that he would sell it when he got into power and get all the money back. Looking back, I can understand it better. Here was a government able to travel around in a plane and here were the people who hardly had roads to walk on. Somare sold it pretty well.

I do not think Somare had any real economic policies – or if he did he preferred to hide them – but the make-up of his government meant he had political support from the Highlands to the coast. While I had Okuk on my team he did not command the respect that other politicians did – even when he gave away about four thousand cartons of beer he still lost the election, and he led the group of Highlanders I depended on. Despite our best efforts, we were defeated by Somare in the 1982 elections and the PPP numbers dropped from about 22 to 16.

I was disappointed to lose because we had to come into government to fix things and we had to suffer the consequences of fixing the country and losing the battle. At the same time, I accepted the political reality – I had lost. The United Party continued its partnership with the Pangu Party and we ended up taking the minority party status again. Michael Somare became Prime Minister for the second time and Paias Wingti became his Deputy Prime Minister.

I found that as a member of the crossbenches I had insufficient things to do, having already sold my share in the shipping company. I did own the Hamamas Hotel in Rabaul but it was always hard to find good managers. The hotel was also burned in a fire but I had no money then to rebuild it. I persuaded a friend, Gerry McGrade, a Scot who used to play football against me in Rabaul, and his wife, Joyce, to buy 50 per cent of the hotel. Gerry rebuilt it and it looked beautiful. But I felt that because of the way I demanded things to be done, my interference in the running of it was an obstacle to him, and so offered him the whole thing, letting him buy me out. Sadly, a volcanic eruption in 1994 severely damaged the hotel but, once again, they rebuilt it. The hotel is now run by his daughter Susie, as Gerry has retired to the Gold Coast in Australia. We are still good friends to this day.

At one time I also had a company called Misimuk, the biggest cigarette distributor in the Papua New Guinea islands. I have always been a hard-working man. I may not have the brains but I have always been able to secure the right people to work for me, people who were smart, hard-working and committed, which meant that I could attend to my political responsibilities. It was at this point I decided to also start an aviation business.

Aviation in the Papua New Guinea islands was very important because although you could depend on shipping and road transport, I wanted to conquer time. I knew a 24-hour boat trip could be reduced to 30 minutes in a helicopter. When we started there was a huge gap in terms of providing a service of this kind and other operators were not very well organised. I began the business by forming a partnership with a New Zealander, David Piddick, who was a helicopter pilot and an engineer. I was the majority owner of the company, Islands Nationair. I had met David when I was Prime Minister and I had used him on occasions. He used to fly helicopters to chase and drop nets on wild deer in New Zealand, which is a very skilled job – only a very capable pilot can fly on those sorts of missions. The New Zealand culture was more tolerant of coloured people because of the Maoris and we were able to talk easily.

I was a silent partner – all I wanted to see was the returns and whether we were able to service our loans. We started out simply, leasing a Jet Ranger helicopter, and from that we started to build up our business in Rabaul. Niugini Mining was coming into the market at this time, particularly in its exploration on Lihir and elsewhere, which meant a lot of work for us – a charter every second or third day was sufficient to keep the business going. In those days a lot of the exploration was in remote areas and the mining companies could get their equipment to the shore but the site might be up on the hill where there were no roads. We would take all the equipment from the beach up to the top of the mountain and became the main method of transport.

Soon after, we bought another Jet Ranger and then a four-blade, rotary-wing helicopter, which could manoeuvre really well. We salvaged a fixed-wing aircraft from a crash site and rebuilt it, and also bought a fixed-wing Islander at auction and repaired it. This latter plane created sufficient income for us to buy another plane and we were the first company to introduce the Long Ranger into Papua New Guinea. The Long Ranger could carry more, and lift more. We also bought three Twin Otters, which is a slow aircraft, a bulldozer of the air, but it can carry up to twenty passengers. We were not really competing with Air Niugini, however, because as a smaller airline focussing on freight we were not in direct competition with them. We just had to find viable routes to stay alive.

It really helped that David was an engineer as he managed to get some of his friends to help him fix the aircraft. After several years we ended up with nine modern helicopters and about fourteen fixed-wing aircraft. Very few aviation companies offered dual rotary and fixed-wing services and we became quite a big operation. I appointed David as Managing Director and I got my sister Louisa to be on the board, while I remained the largest shareholder. Later on David left the company amicably and I got Vanessa to run it for me for a while, until we started to go down in the books. Although she is a very tough woman, somehow the Papua New Guinean pilots did not accept her being in charge, which made it difficult.

I still had my home in Rabaul, my home in Huris, and continued to be the Member for Namatanai. I was a roving member who went from place to place, staying with people, and it was really the physical contact that mattered. Huris is on the eastern side of the island and getting access to the western side of my electorate was important. It was not easy because there were no roads but I could get there more easily from Rabaul, and so I used my airline and the company helicopters to get around. In all those years we did not have a single major incident.

Politically, the years immediately after I left the prime ministership were quiet for me. We used the time to streamline the Constitution of the party and tried to make our policies more real and effective, and we were able to take a position on some very important issues. In 1991 the Constitution was changed to increase, from six months to eighteen, the 'grace' period during which the government could not be dismissed through a parliamentary no-confidence vote. It was argued that the ease with which no-confidence motions could be mounted was creating instability in our political system.

I opposed the idea of an extension because I have always believed that 'stability' can be a stepping stone to dictatorship. That has been shown in every African country where politicians use the legislature to take over power and assume complete control. In Papua New Guinea the government is appointed by the parliament, not like in Australia. Every time we change, we require the elected representatives of the people to nominate who is going to be the alternative Prime Minister. We have to give notice and the parliament gives its authority for a change.

I disagreed with the extension because I believed that six months was already too long for a bad government – they could bankrupt the country in much less time. Stability for the sake of power was not my friend; it has never been my friend. True stability should come only with good governance. Power corrupts and when someone is in power they do not want to relinquish it, which is why absolute power leads to dictatorship. A government should live by the day and constantly earn the respect of the governed.

CHAPTER 14

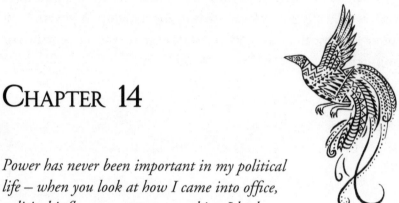

Power has never been important in my political life – when you look at how I came into office, political influence was not something I had really wanted.

Michael Somare remained as Prime Minister until November 1985, when Paias Wingti won a vote of no confidence against him after three attempts – I had been the one who put the first two motions forward but they had both fizzled out. Wingti had been with the Pangu Party before, but had left to form the People's Democratic Movement (PDM). The only way a vote of no confidence can succeed is when there is a split in the government – the division was between Somare, Wingti and Rabbie Namaliu. You know the old saying, 'Oppositions never win – the government loses.' When he was finally defeated, Somare then became the leader of the Opposition.

Wingti had no choice but to invite the PPP to join him because he could not form government otherwise. It was a coalition of parties including the PDM, PPP, National Party, United Party and the Papua Party. I did not have the political numbers to become Prime Minister, to command the majority, so instead I became the Deputy Prime Minister and the Minister for Finance and Planning.

I am adjustable to both leading and being led; I take politics at its real face value. Politically, the party system in Papua New Guinea has never really matured. We never experienced that philosophical divide between socialist and conservative thinking as in Australia or other democracies like the United Kingdom. The basis of the party political system for us was the personality of each leader – they created the parties and organised the way they were able to evoke support. Somare attracted people a lot because he could speak very persuasively, in a conciliatory, almost musical way. He could throw a few nice half-truths in between the political gimmicks and people would fall for them. He also had a very large beard, which made him look mature.

The PPP's messages were not always passed on in a way the people at that time were able to easily absorb. Our ideas may have been a little more intricate than the sweet talk coming from the other politicians. We were a very serious party with policies and a clear goal. That kind of language, however, was not what the people wanted and did not sit as well with the electorate. When it came to election time, it was all about how the party presented its ideas, plans and policies. However, the general population was relatively raw in being able to make its own judgements. We did not carry around our policy papers because very few people could read them. In those days, people in Papua New Guinea liked to look more at pictures than words.

When Wingti took over the government his policy was to 'Look North', meaning Papua New Guinea should embrace greater economic ties with the Asian region. It made sense to connect more with Asia, because of the vast amounts of cheap products made in China – Papua New Guinea needed to look for cheaper sources of supply as Australian goods were expensive. Hong Kong was used as the main shipping base and export centre – about

90 per cent of Chinese goods came via Hong Kong, which at that time was a British colony. They had British free trade sentiments and we had the common language of English.

The goods may not have been of great quality but they were cheap, while Australian standards were very high, as regulatory controls were very strict. As an example, Papua New Guinea was required to import vitamin-enriched rice from Australia. It was very hard for us to import rice from China or India where it had been grown for thousands of years. As a former Trust Territory of Australia, we were required to eat this particular rice, which was only manufactured for Papua New Guinea and was quite expensive.

Diplomatic relations with China had been established very early on in Papua New Guinea's history; in fact, when Somare was first Prime Minister. Albert Maori Kiki was then Foreign Minister and he wrote a special letter of comfort or whatever the diplomatic terminology might be, stating that Taiwan was a province of China. That acknowledgement of the One China policy was embedded in a commitment that continues to this day. While Somare never formally recognised Taiwan he had a lot of personal dealings with people there. It is well known to everybody that the Somare *haus* (house), for instance, in Port Moresby, was co-financed by people in Taiwan.

One issue we had with China was that we were very much against their missile testing in the South Pacific during the 1980s. We protested strongly and the relationship became strained. By the mid-1980s it was quite obvious that China was undergoing a huge and dynamic transition under the guidance of Deng Xiaoping, moving from a communist system to what they called a socialist system, but what was really more a system with capitalist elements. China was very much an underdeveloped country and even now, with all the billions of yuan they have, they still regard themselves as a developing country.

Paias Wingti was one of those young turks who had left university halfway through his course to contest the elections in 1977 – I do not know whether he had finished his studies or not but he probably had greater schooling than I had. He was younger than me – only 34 years old – while I was 38. He was a member of the Jika tribe of the Western Highlands Province but was quite different from many Highlanders. He did not carry that heavy Highlander 'bang' type of impulsive decision-making, although when it was required he would do it. Otherwise he was good to work with, a very smart man who had some good advisors around him and friends in the business world. He was able to assess the presentation of a subject and then make a decision without having to think too much about it. He was really astute.

He was also a businessman in his own right, like me. There is a rule of business that you respect one another and we had no reason to talk falsely to each other. We spoke out authoritatively on issues, made firm decisions and earned each other's respect. Wingti was disciplined and tried to run the government in a sophisticated fashion, more like a business, which meant we were punctual and organised. We worked very well together as in some ways we were quite alike.

My working relationship with Wingti was quite different from the one I'd had with Somare, when I was the Deputy Prime Minister to him. I do not remember whether we had an agreement in writing similar to the Memorandum of Understanding I signed with Somare – I do not believe we did. Wingti seemed to be the kind of person who was true to his word – whatever commitment he gave he would live up to it. Because it was a coalition we all needed one another and, because he was much younger, I did not think that he would do the dirty on me. Wingti had no hesitation in letting me run the show as sometimes he just disappeared for several weeks at a time with his family. He was very casual; he did not really carry power with him although he was big enough to do so. He was just a young man who was naturally able to lead.

It was tough being back in Finance again – I inherited the position from Paul Pora who had been a good businessman, but that did not mean he was a good administrator. We had cash flow problems and the country owed a lot of money – millions – to the suppliers from within. The first thing I had to do was find the best way to release funds so I had to look into short-term borrowing and liquidate all our debts. That was a good move because, once we liquidated the debts in the form of purchase agreements and contracts, the business houses could start to get moving again.

Internationally, this period marked the beginning of the brooding Asian crisis that later broke in 1987 with what became known as Black Monday on 19 October. Stock markets around the world crashed – beginning with Hong Kong – and the trend spread right across Europe and then to the United States. The IMF and the World Bank were just coming in and started to impose their typical economic conditions. We had no choice but to comply because we needed the money – they were very powerful institutions. I remember later, when I took over as Prime Minister again in 1994, they imposed about 25 conditions on Papua New Guinea, which almost choked us completely. At that point it was a question of survival, a time when we were keeping our mouth open to take the last breath. We fought against the conditions and tried to renegotiate but I had to concede to quite a number of World Bank demands.

The floating of shares in the mining company Placer Pacific took place in July 1986. As the Finance Minister it was my responsibility to strike a deal. The stockbroker expressed concerns that Papua New Guinea could not possibly buy the 12.5 million shares put aside for our citizens but, having got the direction from Wingti to not negotiate anything below that allocation, I knew that we had an obligation to fulfil that demand. I had never really dealt with stocks and shares before; in fact, that was the first time I had encountered them. Many leading figures bought shares, including the Chief Justice Buri Kidu, but mine were perceived to be a little bit more sinful than others because I was the Finance Minister and I bought a big parcel under advice from my lawyer, Julian Thirlwall. I borrowed money and bought about 15,000 shares. I did not make very much money, about 30 toea a share, because I did not keep them for long as I was worried about the repayment of the loan I had taken out.

When the story appeared in the media, it was published in a way that was quite embarrassing. There was the connotation that the Finance Minister was using public money to buy shares for himself and his family. It did a lot of damage to me personally and caused a lot of distress within my family, although we did everything right. After an inquiry, when the ruling was handed down, Justice Timothy Hinchcliffe stated that at all relevant times I had acted in the best interest of the people of Papua New Guinea.

Wingti also tried very hard to resolve the existing disquiet on Bougainville, although I was really concentrating more on restoring stability to the economy. Wingti did a lot to try to establish contact with Bougainvilleans and he had members in his party from Bougainville, such as Michael Ogio, who later became the Governor-General. They all tried to establish a better dialogue but they probably did not give the issue enough attention at the time.

Another issue that continued to fester followed on from the Indonesian government's decision in 1984 to seize traditionally owned land for transmigration sites, causing thousands of West Papuans to cross the border to seek refuge in Papua New Guinea. Very soon after I had become Prime Minister in 1980, President Suharto invited me to Indonesia. I found Suharto and all his ministers to be very calm, cool, collected and co-operative. In my view the Indonesians are very polite people, very considerate. They have a culture of immense patience and humility, or at least it radiated that way from the leaders to the people.

The issue with Irian Jaya, now known as West Papua, relates back to the early 1960s when the superpowers, for their own good reasons, made the decision, approved by the US Kennedy government, that Indonesia would take over West Papua. The 'Act of Free Choice' in 1969 cemented Indonesian control. From then on the people were divided by the border. We had begun to deal with this problem in small ways around the time of Independence. Before that it was an Australian problem.

When they started this transmigration scheme there were a lot of incursions from Indonesian soldiers into Papua New Guinea. We had about 60 markers – signposts for the divisions between the two states – along the 1000-kilometre border through some of the roughest terrain you would ever find anywhere in the world. I imagine the markers were made of cement and there were so few that it was not possible to blame people for not being able to see where the border was marked, and so naturally they crossed it. The cultures on both sides of the border are one and the same, so movement is quite common. I regard people living on the Indonesian side of the border as Papua New Guineans;

I see them as West Sepik as they are almost identical. Ethnically, they are Papua New Guineans but, in terms of citizenship, they are not.

There were times when the issue began to intensify, particularly when the Indonesians wanted to flush out all the Organisasi Papua Merdeka (OPM), or the Free Papua Organisation, rebels. In many instances the Indonesian soldiers followed the OPM in hot pursuit across the border. Both sides had been very careful not to arrest people crossing the border, especially military personnel. During my first prime ministership, I was caught in a situation where the incursions became too frequent. I needed to let the Indonesians know they were doing it too much – they were doing it to their own citizens who did not like them and they were doing it to a country that had its own status. We had a border agreement so I made it clear they should observe it. Our policy was that whoever was caught violating the border would be dealt with accordingly.

Wingti faced this issue when he was Prime Minister and it also arose again later when I was in office for the second time. I issued an order to capture whoever violated the border, although that did not happen because we did not have the resources. We may have captured one or two OPM members but at the same time we were somewhat hesitant to capture the Indonesian soldiers. Papua New Guinea would just run out of bullets if Indonesia ever decided to march across the border.

I do not think that they will ever do anything to cause a deterioration in their relationship with us. They've got enough islands of their own; they are quite self-sufficient. I personally do not think it is in their minds to cross the border, although we have to constantly be on guard about it. Taking over Papua New Guinea would be a liability for Indonesia, while taking over

125

Australia would be a real asset. We solve the problem for Australia by making certain that Indonesia does not do that. I do not think this issue will flare up in my lifetime, but we cannot know. It will depend on the leadership at the time.

By 1985 we had been independent for ten years. There had been many gains made during this decade and if the country was not as far ahead as it might have been, the blame did not lie so much with the system or the personalities involved but with the nature of the policies and the policymakers. One issue that was of increasing concern was the escalation of general law and order problems in Port Moresby and in some of the larger towns. Of course Papua New Guinea has always had tribal wars, which are essentially small-scale civil wars. They are usually contained and quite traditional, so no one outside those communities really talks about or worries about them a great deal. If I took history as a guide, then I would argue that there has been a huge reduction in the number of tribal fights in the past 40 years.

After Independence, the country had started to change course and a lot more people were moving from the rural provinces into the cities and towns. The police and the PNGDF were also struggling to manage themselves. They had become used to receiving a significant amount of guidance from external advisors in Australia, but in the years following Independence this support was gradually reduced or removed entirely. There was a general rise of what became known as the rascal gangs, or *raskolism*, which became a phrase a lot of people used to describe the kinds of crimes that were taking place.

This rise in crime was coupled with the fear of our capability to run the government and people began to concentrate a lot more on security issues and how they would survive. There were more and more break and enters, and a slight rise in the number of incidents that involved crime-related killings. My view, however, is that the rise of *raskols* was simply a new era of nation-building. I do not know a great deal of detail about how other nations were created, but some of them went through terrible civil wars while Papua New Guinea had one of the best transitions of any country at that time. I do not want to ignore the fact that there was an increase in crime rates, but I also think that if we had been able to compare those figures to levels before Independence then we would confirm that the rise was not that big, and the nature of those offences was not so different from what had existed before.

One main factor in the rise of crime was, of course, the growing number of squatter settlements in places like Port Moresby and Lae, and the difficulties people then faced in trying to survive away from their own land and gardens and out of reach of their own communities. They came to settle rather than return so they quickly became not just itinerant visitors but more or less refugee settlers. At this time around Port Moresby there was enough land – Crown land and traditionally owned land – for people to just go and pick the place they liked because the city was not crowded. That was how the settlements at places like Six Mile and Nine Mile built up, because the government land was not occupied. People even started settling right in the heart of Koki and at the bottom of Three Mile Hill – I remember there were tents there and that situation helped to breed the problems.

The reaction from many people in the community was to increase security. The fences came up initially among people who could afford to put up a fence. It reflected the sense of personal concern about safety and a natural instinct by people to protect themselves. There were serious break and enters, there was no doubt about that, but there were not large numbers of criminals carrying rifles or anything like that. We were also going through

127

a period where the media was becoming more significant – they represented new ways of communication. More newspapers and radio stations were coming in so people were starting to be better informed. Before, when a serious crime was committed, the victim would just be chopped up and thrown in a grave somewhere and nobody would know anything about it. People now learned how to take out advertisements in the newspapers, often quite large ones, about the deaths of people and how that person had been killed.

At one point there were quite a few expatriates leaving Papua New Guinea because of all the negative media, and I sometimes wondered whether those who were well established spread the word of terror because they wanted to contain opportunities for themselves. Every crisis has the effect of stopping too much new competition coming in.

Naturally some people think that as Prime Minister I had millions of kina just lying around for criminals to break in and take. Back in the early 1980s not too many people had large security fences surrounding their homes like they do today – I certainly did not have one when I was broken into. But gradually criminals were becoming more organised. This meant that when they saw bars on the windows, they just brought a car jack and broke the bars apart. Actually, I thought it was quite smart of them to do that. In fact, I borrowed that skill one time at Huris, when the house began to dip because one of the posts was sinking into an old bomb hole. I filled up the bottom with cement and used a jack to prop up the post. Even though I do not favour criminals in any way, I learned something useful from that break-in.

Chapter 15

It seemed no one grasped the enormity of what was happening on Bougainville; it was not something that had got into the bones of the decision-makers, even though it had been brewing for some time.

In 1986 I became the Minister for Trade and Industry under Paias Wingti, continuing to serve as Deputy Prime Minister. There was a trade policy I wished to pursue with Australia because I wanted to change the emphasis between us from aid to trade. I tried to suggest a formula but it did not sink into Australian minds, or they just had a blank head at that time.

I spoke at the Canberra Press Club on the subject of trade not aid. I suggested we create some form of special preferential trade agreement between Papua New Guinea, as well as all the developing countries in the Pacific, and Australia. I thought Australia could import all our copra and cocoa at an economic price to keep the countries in the Pacific happy – a stabilisation scheme that would help support and contain people in their respective independent islands instead of having a big flow of Cook Islanders, Nauruans and Samoans into Australia and New Zealand.

I thought I was doing Australia a favour by proposing this but it was not put on their agenda at all. It was hard to persuade them because they had a very laissez-faire attitude towards planning, particularly economic planning. At the time they simply reacted to the circumstances. They were not like the Chinese, who planned for certain things. The European countries and the Commonwealth allowed former colonies access to their market without any duties but Australia never provided anything like that. Even the lengthy requirement for the processing of our visas from Papua New Guinea to Australia suggested to me that they were not a good post-colonial partner.

Australia just did not have the kind of attitude or experience you might find in other countries that are less paternalistic in their attitudes towards their former colonies. For example, I thought Australia should give working preference to crop and fruit pickers from the Pacific – something that has happened more since 2004 after I became Chairman of the Eminent Persons Group in the Pacific Islands Forum. That Eminent Persons Group was very impressive and included the Chancellor of the University of the South Pacific and the Ombudsman of Samoa. These sorts of deals are happening a little bit more now – hopefully Australia is becoming more mature in its outlook.

Wingti led the government through the elections of July 1987 but was defeated in a vote of no confidence in June 1988. Rabbie Namaliu, who had recently assumed the leadership of the Pangu Party from Michael Somare, became the fourth Prime Minister of the country. Before he went into politics Namaliu had been an academic at the University of Papua New Guinea. He was different from Somare and although they both came from a higher school of learning, Namaliu concentrated more on presenting written policies whereas Somare focussed more on verbal policies. Namaliu was very articulate, capable, and sometimes he spoke a little bit above people, as though he was perhaps in cloud six or seven. I do not think he was decisive enough during his prime ministership and because of his academic background he thought a lot before he made a decision, and sometimes there were no decisions at all.

In 1989 the problems on Bougainville erupted when militants blew up the pylons supplying electricity to the Panguna copper mine and demanded billions of dollars in compensation from Bougainville Copper Limited (BCL). This signalled the effective end of large-scale mining on Bougainville. Before this, militants had committed several acts of arson but the sabotage of the power supply was organised by former soldier Sam Kauona, who had left the army to work for the head of the Bougainville Revolutionary Army (BRA), Francis Ona. The blowing up of the pylons was done by people who had been trained to do it. The government's attitude was: 'Well, it has been blown up. We can repair it again and BCL will fix it.'

If I had been involved in mining, I might have taken this act of sabotage to be incredibly serious, but I do not think that we in parliament knew enough about the extent of the damage to consider it a major problem. We thought it was an isolated incident. No one could guess that the situation would develop the way it did. Economically the mine was important to Papua New Guinea but no one was looking specifically at that issue. In the minds of many, the mine was instigated by the Australian government and was very much an Australian investment in the country.

Somare's attitude and philosophy towards the Bougainville issue had been that if you allowed a problem to stay for long enough it would probably solve itself, and Namaliu had a similar outlook. Because there was no immediate reaction in a pragmatic and substantial way, the matter was allowed to develop in an opposite direction, and this became the status quo. In this particular case, BCL should have taken much more corrective action to deal with the situation.

Mining operations formally ceased in May 1989. The government declared a State of Emergency on Bougainville in June of the same year and decided to send in troops to stop the uprising. The Bougainvilleans were not surprised when the troops arrived; they must have expected it. However, the soldiers did not really enforce the law in the strongest possible sense, meaning not to kill people but to take the matter through the legal process. What we should have done was to go in, take the culprits out, deal with them lawfully and try to restore respect for the rule of law. If we had gone in more seriously, the way the PNGDF had gone into Vanuatu in 1980, then the outcome might have been different. I do not think the PNGDF going into Bougainville had any clear directions at all; they did not know who the enemies were, or fully understand the circumstances. Our troops were totally unprepared and it was a completely disastrous deployment.

The issue was that Bougainvilleans wanted a fairer deal, a better acknowledgement of the fact that they were part of the land that produced the wealth. It was really just as simple as that. It all boiled down to this one thing and right from the start we knew what it was, we were just not able to address it. It should have been a simple exercise of reviewing the mining agreement and giving the locals the right to what they had been standing on for almost 40,000 years. To the Bougainvilleans, land was like religion and the opening of the mine was like an enforced change. You cannot turn a Catholic away from what he believes in and say, 'No, you have to take on these other beliefs because the Methodists think that way.' Those values are ingrained. Land on Bougainville, as in all of Papua New Guinea, is life.

Several soldiers died during those early months. Every time Prime Minister Rabbie Namaliu went to the airport he was paying homage to another dead soldier, policeman or government official, and he was photographed in tears. I am not too sure how the Bougainvilleans interpreted this but it could have been seen as defeatist in attitude. A military blockade was also imposed around Bougainville to stop the inflow of arms from the Solomon Islands, using the short sea crossing between the two countries. The blockade was necessary just to stop the interference from outside.

It was only a matter of months before the government negotiated a ceasefire with the BRA on the condition that the troops would be withdrawn and that Namaliu would release some detainees. It marked a turn in events as the BRA looked at the withdrawal of our troops as a victory, without question. It gave the BRA an advantage and not long after they were able to dominate the area around the mine, following the old warrior ways where one side takes the highest position so they can see if their enemy is approaching.

Many Bougainvilleans had lost a lot of their kin, their friends, and they believed this was because of the intervention by the military. Their attitude would have been: 'Had we been able to look after ourselves as we have for so many thousands of years, this would not have happened.' Everything was blamed on the national government. Our own military then began to develop resentment, because they too had lost a lot of friends and began to look at Bougainvilleans as the enemy.

At the time of the decision to withdraw, Paul Tohian was the Commissioner for Police. The initial engagement of the PNGDF had come about because of the State of Emergency imposed, under which the PNGDF was placed in the control of the police force. Tohian adamantly opposed the withdrawal. He was half Bougainvillean and a strong law enforcer – his father had also been a very high-ranking policeman so he had been brought up in that way of thinking. At first he refused to get out of Bougainville because of his reasoning and assimilation with the people – he probably knew about their temperament more than anybody. His attitude was: 'If you go in you should finish the job.'

His view was that a pullback was a defeat, especially so by the state against a small section of its own people, which had ramifications not just for Bougainville but for the rest of the country. When the government and the police force were seen to be not serious about enforcing the law, it had a big impact. As a result of that episode Tohian, who was in Port Moresby, then said he was going to overthrow the government – he was either high or drunk when he said it. I remember when that happened. I rang up Namaliu and told him to take extra precautions and I rang Somare too, to tell him what I had heard. Even though I was in the Opposition, I thought of them as friends and did not want anything to happen to them. There was quite a lot of disruption in the police force when news of the possible overthrow of the government became known. After everyone sobered up, everything calmed down and fell back into line, which is the Melanesian way. Tohian was then removed from his post.

Namaliu was surrounded by people like Michael Somare and Ted Diro, and they had probably talked him into conceding to the withdrawal of troops. Maybe he was making decisions on too many issues at the same time. Whatever his reasons, that decision was the downfall of all governments thereafter.

I have never been able to allow a suspicion in my mind to fade away that Rio Tinto allowed the situation on Bougainville to deteriorate because the price of copper was very low at that time. They had several mines in Africa that were not doing well and I suspected they did not want to bring one of the biggest concentrations in the world onto the market because the international copper price had gone down. If I had been in the mining business I would have provided all the security necessary to protect the mine; I would have helped the government in any way possible, especially if I had the might of Rio Tinto. They could have engaged the resources of a company like Sandline but they did not. They just walked away, slowly and silently, and disappeared from the scene. It was surprising, very surprising.

I am not prepared to say that Rio Tinto allowed the situation to deteriorate deliberately but as a thinker, as a manager, as a normal businessman, I could not help but wonder about how funny it was that they did not treat the matter more seriously. BCL will never want to let go of Bougainville because they know it still holds enormous economic value.

CHAPTER 16

It has been a long tradition among many prime ministers who regard another senior minister as a political threat to put that minister in Foreign Affairs.

After the elections in July 1992, the new parliament elected Paias Wingti for his second term of office – he beat Rabbie Namaliu by a margin of only one vote. Namaliu and Somare went back to the Opposition benches. Masket Iangalio became Minister for Mining and Petroleum, and I became, once again, Minister for Finance and Planning. As Minister for Finance I was directed in 1993 to replace Henry ToRobert, the first Governor of our Central Bank. He had been in the position since 1973 and was only a few months short of reaching his twentieth anniversary. I would really have loved to have seen him complete the period. I was told to replace him with Mekere Morauta and so I had the unfortunate task of telling ToRobert.

In 1993 I also celebrated my twenty-fifth year of political life. My father came from Sydney to Port Moresby for a function that was held to mark the occasion. At the dinner I remember very clearly my father leaning over to speak to me privately – in fact, I have a photograph of that very moment – and because he was deaf, he made sure he got very close to my ear to whisper to me. He leaned in and said, 'You should give up. You've done enough. Get out of politics. Do not trust the army, the police. I do not like politics. You should leave now; you've done your job. You should come back and run your business.' Those were my father's last memorable words to me. It just so happened that the Sandline affair followed a few years afterwards so he predicted those things before they happened.

My mother's words had kept me going in my political life whereas my father had a different message. He put a big question mark on my continuing commitment – I probably should have listened to him. He had always thought a little bit differently to me on politics, and he always wanted me to go back into the family business.

Under Wingti's leadership we became more involved in international affairs, particularly in terms of developing our financial institutions. I travelled quite a bit to promote Papua New Guinea in different forums. In September 1993 I was in the Bahamas for a Finance Minister's conference when I heard that Wingti had secretly resigned and then, on the next sitting day of parliament, the Speaker of the National Parliament, Bill Skate, immediately asked for nominations for Prime Minister as the first order of business. Skate was the leader of the People's National Congress, which had entered into a coalition partnership with Wingti's People's Democratic Movement. Most of the members in the House were taken completely by surprise by the move, and some Opposition members walked out. Because of this Wingti was re-elected unopposed. Wingti had now been Prime Minister for around fifteen months. This was a clever tactical move on his part to create a 'new' government that could not be challenged by a no-confidence motion for another eighteen months.

I did not know anything about it at the time. I subsequently learned the decision was made quite abruptly and following advice from some of Wingti's lawyers. Skate was somehow involved in it and even the Governor-General. They just made the decision and it appeared to be acceptable but there was no interpretation of the constitutionality of it or whether it had properly followed conventions and procedure. It was a very, very clever act but my immediate thought was that it was wrong.

Even though I was his deputy, I did not think that Wingti's decision was something he needed to consult me about. It may have related to the economic situation, where the government was seeking an increase in the state's direct involvement in the mining industry. Bob Needham, who had been the Managing Director of Placer Pacific at the time of its controversial share float, was now advising Wingti, as were a few other people. At this point Papua New Guinea was home to several major mining projects: the Ok Tedi mine in Western Province, the gold and silver mine on Misima Island in Milne Bay Province, the Kutubu oil project in the Southern Highlands, and the Porgera gold and silver mining operation in Enga Province.

There were also probably some outside parties with pecuniary interests who were also trying to retain Wingti as Prime Minister. I certainly think there were more economic pressures than political ones in the decision-making and perhaps there were other hidden reasons. Here was a Prime Minister who had resigned and been re-elected, and in the process was prepared to test the Constitution. However, there were a lot of protests that the move was unconstitutional. A large number of people marched on parliament demanding the resignation of Wingti, Skate and the Governor-General Sir Wiwa Korowi.

Opposition leader Chris Haiveta soon filed a court challenge to Wingti's re-election. I was in a position then to allow the court to decide, because I too needed a very clear explanation of the legality of the situation. In November 1993, the court challenge failed but was immediately appealed. It was then just a question of waiting to see what the outcome of the court case would be.

Around this time our monetary reserve was not strong. We were very short of funds. As the Finance Minister I sought a deal from the Union Bank of Switzerland. They did not want a country guarantee from us; they wanted a resource guarantee on our mining and petroleum revenues, which would have normally been directed to the Mineral Resources Stabilisation Fund. I had to guarantee our borrowing for a generation of our resources. I thought there was nothing wrong with the deal, that it wouldn't matter whether we repaid the loan through resource-generated revenue or sovereign guarantee, so I approved it.

Foreign Affairs Ministers are usually those people who the Prime Minister wants to make sure are not in the country to disturb them all the time. In January 1994, not long after his re-election, I was appointed Foreign Affairs Minister and replaced as Minister for Finance by Masket Iangalio. I never saw myself as a threat to Wingti but perhaps some other people did. It was possible that Wingti regarded me as a contender and a likely successor but I did not think this was a major concern of his. However, the truth is Wingti did not remove me as Finance Minister; it was my wish to move on. I felt it was the right time for me and I wanted the Foreign Affairs portfolio. I felt that it would be a more appropriate opportunity for me to educate myself in the forms of governments other leaders used to run their respective countries.

I had already been Finance Minister three or four times and I was really looking forward to a change. Every time I had been Finance Minister I went through a lot of stresses and strains and by 1993 we were beginning to go through a series of international interventions, particularly with the World Bank. I felt I had reached a saturation point with finance. As Papua New Guinea was growing up, sooner or later we would have a demand to liaise more with the Pacific countries. The South Pacific was such a vast area and I was not going to allow the distance to prevent our influence and ability to establish stronger relationships.

When I became the Foreign Affairs Minister I used the government aircraft, *The Kumul*, to travel around. I was probably the only person who had ever travelled to all the countries in the South Pacific territories. I started at Port Moresby and went to Vanimo, Palau, the Federated States of Micronesia and then to Tuvalu, Kiribati, Solomon Islands, Fiji, Tonga, Samoa, Eastern Samoa, Western Samoa – all these countries. I covered them all in that little aircraft.

In May 1994 thousands of Papua New Guinean landowners, represented by the Australian law firm Slater and Gordon, took out a K2.7 billion lawsuit in Melbourne against Broken Hill Proprietary Ltd (BHP), the majority shareholder and operating partner of the Ok Tedi mine in Western Province. These mining companies operated like a territory of their own and were isolated and a long way away from Port Moresby. Western Province, the largest province in the country, covers almost 100,000 square kilometres and sits on the border with Indonesia. The landowners claimed that their rivers, the Fly in particular, had been damaged because of the enormous amount of tailings from the mine – estimated to be up to 100,000 tonnes every day. They were seeking compensation for environmental damage.

The question of the environment was quite a new thing in Papua New Guinea. People had always seen dirty water after a heavy downpour and it was too early for us to even realise the effect of cyanide in the water. How can a Papua New Guinean living in the bush know anything about that? At Ok Tedi, however, the excessive build-up of waste had started to kill the vegetation. People in that region relied on crops such as sago, bananas and taro to survive but the discharge of the tailings caused flooding and left behind contaminated mud in the gardens. It was only when the gardens at the edge of the river started to be affected and people began to see dead fish that they chose to complain.

By the time of the lawsuit, the whole of the Fly River was polluted. The impact of the class action did wake everybody up a little. I am not quite sure, as a government, whether we were supporting Slater and Gordon. We wanted to assist the people but not in the type of legal onslaught for which Slater and Gordon was known. They were not really good friends of the government at that time. Clearly we did not want Ok Tedi to pollute the waters – we wanted to protect the livelihoods of our people – but the country needed the revenue from the mine. Eventually there was an out-of-court settlement between BHP and the landowners and the majority share ownership was later transferred from BHP to the PNG Sustainable Development Program. It was a way out for BHP.

The general mining industry at the time was almost coming to a standstill in terms of total exploration in Papua New Guinea. In hindsight, we gave too many concessions to bring the mining companies in. We had made some very, very big mistakes in

1992, during the prime ministership of Rabbie Namaliu, when we changed the mining law to take away the ownership from the customary landowners. The new *Mining Act* gave the state ownership of 'all minerals existing on, in or below the surface of any land ... including any minerals contained in any water lying on any land in Papua New Guinea'.

The *Mining Act 1992* was a flow-on from the fact that there was no exploration, no new investment on the horizon. Papua New Guinea, so rich in minerals, needed incentives to attract investment in exploration work. If the system was changed a little to encourage more investment, that would have been regarded as reasonable. Even though the bureaucracy had been thinking about a revised law for some time, in my view the public service was too raw – in that industry the new law was guided entirely by those big companies. The issues were: we had to get our economy back on track and we had to put Papua New Guinea back on the credibility map by resolving the Bougainville issue. In many instances the environmental impact issues were just put on hold or shelved. It was the question of revenue that was foremost in the mind of the government at that time.

As we were meeting at the 25th South Pacific Forum in Brisbane in August 1994, the government launched Operation High Speed, an ambitious move by the PNGDF to recapture the Panguna copper mine. The assault was backed up by helicopter support, which brought in more troops and essential supplies. At first the BRA allowed the troops to establish their positions but they soon launched their counterattack and the PNGDF suffered many casualties.

Meanwhile we were still waiting for the results of the constitutional challenge to Wingti's re-election. Naturally, in the game of politics, I needed to be prepared and have a strategy.

I was therefore in contact with other political parties. As the date of the Supreme Court ruling approached in August, a lot of tension came in – bush lawyers started to talk about the way the decision might go. I was the logical person to take the prime ministership because I was already Deputy Prime Minister. I had been a reliable deputy but I had to be prepared to continue the government without Wingti.

On Thursday, 25 August, the Supreme Court ruled that while Wingti's resignation had been valid, his re-election had not. The court also ruled that Wingti was now the interim Prime Minister and that a new election must be held on the next sitting day of parliament, which was five days later on Tuesday, 30 August 1994, the day after my 55th birthday.

The PPP had been holding its annual conference that weekend and a resolution was passed supporting my nomination for the prime ministership. I had the support of Chris Haiveta, who was now heading the Pangu Party, and Wingti had decided not to stand for re-election. Bill Skate resigned as Speaker and was replaced by former Prime Minister Rabbie Namaliu. With all these accumulated problems, the country was going through a period of uncertainty and there was a lot of support for my bid so we could stabilise the country.

It was probably a choice between me, Michael Somare or Chris Haiveta, but Haiveta was not really ready to take on the leadership at this time. Somare had broken away from Pangu and had formed the National Alliance Party with Bernard Narokobi, Moi Avei, Bart Philemon and Masket Iangalio. The National Alliance later went on to do very well at the 2002 elections, winning government. They stayed there for the full five-year term, making that government the first since Independence to survive a full term without a vote of no confidence.

The whole of parliament was geared up and ready for the vote. Skate was the only person who stood against me but he was not a serious contender. Skate may have had a motive in standing for the prime ministership, I do not know. He may have wanted to crucify Wingti as he had been heavily involved in Wingti's resignation. We already knew what the decision would be and I was ready. I was elected Prime Minister again, I believe, by 65 votes to 32.

Chapter 17

The loss of Rabaul was devastating – it was the root of all my business, from shipping and aviation to hotels, everything.

I knew I faced a series of challenges when I became Prime Minister for the second time. The first and most important item on my agenda was the Bougainville secession crisis, where the Panguna mine currently lay dormant. We also had a debt crisis because in the nine months that Masket Iangalio had been Finance Minister our reserves had gone right down – he simply spent a lot of money we did not have.

I turned my attention first to Bougainville. I did not think the lost revenue from that area was the central issue but the ongoing crisis was damaging to the country and over $100 million a year was being spent on Bougainville, defence and other costs. We also had to restore tranquillity to restore our reputation. That was another reason why I wanted to bring about an end to the crisis, which had also inflamed pre-existing tensions between different groups on the island. Bougainville was the centrepoint of all our problems. My view was that, one way or another, I had to find a resolution.

By the time I came into office we had lost thousands of people in Bougainville through direct killings, disease and premature deaths. No one really knows exactly how many people died – even to this day. It was a very bad chapter of our country's history. Many years later we were to spend millions investigating incidents, such as the tragic sinking of the *Rabaul Queen* off the coast of Morobe Province in 2012. That was the right thing to do because more than 160 people died in that disaster. However, we have never really clarified how many people died in the Bougainville conflict; it seemed the rest of the country did not really care and even now many people seem to prefer to forget this.

As soon as I came into office I made it clear there was a new motto: 'A new deal for Bougainville.' Within 48 hours I travelled to the Solomon Islands and met with the Commander of the Bougainville Revolutionary Army (BRA), Sam Kauona. I wanted to generate some kind of recognition and comfort to them, to say, 'Look, it is a new ballgame. I am prepared to deal with you but let us play by rules we can both respect.'

On 4 September 1994 we signed the Honiara Agreement, which paved the way for a ceasefire, a lifting of the military blockade and for the convening of a pan-Bougainville peace conference within five weeks. Thereafter, I kept on getting the Bougainvillean leaders who were willing to meet us to come to Port Moresby. We organised for the peace conference to be held in the capital of Bougainville, Arawa, that October and I was able to finally bring to fruition my vision of a regional peacekeeping force. It had taken me so many years – since the Vanuatu crisis of 1980 – to get to this point. I deliberately arranged for a Tongan, Colonel Fetu Tupou, to lead the peacekeepers as the Chief of Operations. He was very good. Australia, New Zealand, Fiji and Vanuatu also supported us, providing infantry troops. The exercise became known as Operation Lagoon. I asked the peacekeeping force to keep a distance from both sides. I wanted them to do their best to take the middle road.

We sent a helicopter to collect BRA leader Francis Ona from the mountain at Panguna to bring him down to the peace talks. Everything was arranged. The peacekeeping troops were doing a great job, everyone was ready, but Ona would not come. Even though this was a disappointment, of course, there was still a breakthrough at the talks. The peacekeeping forces escorted BRA Regional Commander Ishmael Toroama to the talks and I was also able to start a dialogue with Theodore Miriung, who was subsequently elected as the leader of the new Bougainville Transitional Government.

At the same time all this was going on, less than three weeks after I took office, a terrible disaster occurred. On 19 September two volcanoes in Rabaul, Tavurvur and Vulcan, suddenly erupted. There had been a bit of rumbling before but that had passed and no one was too concerned. This time, however, we had begun to worry because the Matupit people, whose village was close to Tavurvur, started to walk out of their homes and through the town of Rabaul. Dogs were barking and the roosters were crowing at odd times, and so nature was telling us that something real was going to happen.

The day after the eruption I flew to Rabaul on board *The Kumul* with Rabbie Namaliu, who was the Speaker of the House and the Member for Kokopo. We landed at Tokua Airport, about 40 kilometres southeast of Rabaul. We could not get to Rabaul or anywhere near it because the ash and dust had been blowing up to 18,000 metres and the pilot was very worried. By then the town had been evacuated, the airport was destroyed and most of the town was covered in layers of thick ash. The damage was so bad that whole buildings had collapsed under the weight.

My wife, Stella, had been in Port Moresby at the time so the only person staying at our house was our son Byron. As soon as the volcano erupted Byron tried to rescue our belongings. He was looking after the cigarette distributorship of our company Misimuk, and about K20,000 was in the safe. When Byron saw all the people walking out of Rabaul, he was so moved by their plight that he took all my money and gave it away to the people to buy food.

I was still involved in the aviation business at this time – we had a big hangar and our own terminal right next to the volcano. As the eruptions increased, a decision was made to fly the aircraft out of Rabaul. They took off at midnight and went to Kavieng, all of them, like a military invasion. Kavieng did not have any provisions for night flying but they used torches on the airstrip and fortunately the skies were clear that night.

I then returned to Port Moresby but about a week later I went back to Rabaul to inspect the damage. My house, like many others, was completely in pieces and I could not recognise it; all my belongings, everything was gone. The only thing that I could see was the cement tank I had built for our water catchment at the back of the house. I had put a room on top of that, where my mother used to live. That was all I could see. The eruptions totally dislocated our business and we lost a lifetime spent in the family home. Within a few days everything we had was gone – it was really tough.

It was a great source of sadness to me that the whole community of Rabaul had been so devastated. It was probably the friendliest town in the country. The multi-racial community were nice, tolerant people, and that was probably the reason why so few were hurt or killed. The planning and evacuation drills had also helped keep the death toll low because everyone knew what to do. As the town had a long history of actual and threatened eruptions that meant emergency services were well prepared – I believe only a handful of people died and one of those was because he refused to move. Rabaul had gone through an eruption before in 1937 and then the Japanese came during the war – all these things had probably made the Rabaul people spontaneously respond to the threat.

Commercial ships in the area made several rescue missions to pick up stranded villagers and thousands of people fled to Kokopo and other villages or to the Catholic mission at Vunapope. We were helped enormously by the PNGDF and the assistance of other countries that sent emergency relief supplies. The eruptions resulted in a huge number of people leaving Rabaul permanently. They were not even going to resettle in Kokopo but were taking their businesses somewhere else. I would say about 60 per cent of the business people went within the first two weeks. They probably had nothing left, as in my case. The office, the terminal, the hangar, everything was submerged. What we were able to salvage was very little, just a few spare parts.

We declared a State of Emergency and once this was announced the police went in. There was talk of looting but I looked at that in a different way. It was never a thorn for me as the leader of the government – I saw those people as salvaging rather than looting. What was the use of having all this food left around when it was going to be rotten within the next 24 hours? It was about survival, not theft. Even though there was a restoration committee, the Gazelle Restoration Authority, everything positive grew out of the natural co-operative spirit of the Tolai people. They have a special gift for looking after one another. It was the human element of success.

*

Nine days after the Rabaul volcano erupted, my father died. If he was sick he never told me. That was his make-up – he never revealed his weaknesses. Each time I visited him in Sydney, I would take him out to a restaurant and he would always appear to be fine during the time I spent with him. In the end he just went to sleep and passed away, a pretty natural death. I am not sure exactly how old he was when he died but we think about 98 and he was still very strong. In a sense, although it was a surprise, it was not a shock to me.

My father was an important figure in my life and I knew he had to go one day. He was ageing and I was quite satisfied that I had given everything I could to him. My brother Michael was with him when he died, as was my stepmother, Yee Kun Chin. Michael's family had been living in Sydney since the Rabaul volcano because his wife, Maria, had to have dialysis. When Michael and I split the family shipping business during my first prime ministership, he ended up buying a unit in Earlwood. Our agreement was that my father would be able to live there, without any costs, for the rest of his life.

I flew down for the service, which was held at St Joseph's in Hunters Hill. My father was buried at a cemetery in Ryde, Sydney. His gravestone reads: 'In loving memory of our dearest father, Bernard Chin Pak, died September 28th 1994. "Treasure him O Lord, in your garden of rest."' I go there every year on the anniversary of his death, just like I have visited my mother's grave every year since 1974 on the anniversary of her death. I also do the same for my stepmother, Yee Kun Chin, who died on 21 September 1998, almost four years after my father. She was buried at a cemetery outside Brisbane, where she had moved to live with her son, Bosco, after my father's death. I always go there because it is natural for me to do so. The plaque on her grave reads: 'In loving memory of our beloved mother, Yee Kun Chin, who passed away 21–9–1998, aged 87 years. Always remembered.' I will keep going to their graves until I am forced to stop.

What is life? It's very simple. There must be something more significant and important than daily work. I cut all the business of the world on those days just so that I can be at my parents' graves. It's my duty.

Chapter 18

*Almost twenty years after Independence it was
clear that the provincial government system was
not running well.*

When I came back into office there was an urgent need to deal
with Papua New Guinea's immediate financial problems and the
wider issues in the economy. In just that one nine-month period
Masket Iangalio had been Finance Minister we had spent three
times more than during the same period of the year before. I
appointed Chris Haiveta as the Finance Minister but, during that
initial phase, I had to look after the money problems more than
Chris as he needed to adjust to the job. This was not because I had
more experience, but because I felt I had that initial responsibility
of this new government.

During 1994 there had been a drop in foreign exchange
earnings, some capital flight, and overspending, as well as other
mismanagement, which had led to a drop in the value of the kina.
One morning I was woken up about five o'clock by the Governor
of the Central Bank, Koiari Tarata, a very capable man whom
I had appointed when I came into office as a replacement for
Mekere Morauta. He told me that our reserve had completely

dried up, that we were practically bankrupt. I had not seen that coming.

We had actually gone into a negative currency reserve in the Central Bank. We had to get out of that situation because the business houses were watching us all the time. They knew that the reserve was going down, that the currency was about to collapse. They were paying import orders ahead of actually getting the goods as well as exporting their funds. Money that was being earned from the exports of our products, including gold and minerals, was being kept offshore. I had to intervene and I had very little choice. Our credibility was gone and we did not have any money to buy more imports. We had to do something to stop a sudden outflow of money because we had started to put the brake on, which could have caused an even bigger outflow and a crisis of confidence in the government.

I immediately devalued the kina by about 12 per cent, a substantial drop. Even then the money was not coming in to rebuild the reserve. I had no choice then but to stop all banking. I closed down all banks for one week just to give me time to adjust. Thereafter, I allowed trading to take place depending on a daily income to offset the imports. That was how we planned to slowly get ourselves out of the situation. There was a reaction from the international business houses, although they certainly knew the reason behind what we'd done, and that was why they had kept the money offshore – they were just as responsible for the situation as the country itself.

Because of my experience, somehow we were able to slow down, address the lack of confidence in the government and gradually work ourselves out of the situation. There was a lot of explaining to do and I tried my best to do this. Closing down all bank trading for one whole week – this was the kind of thing that had rarely been done. We had to take some very, very tough measures and we decided to float the kina that October in order to strengthen the position of our international reserves. Right throughout the whole history of PNG's currency movements – from the dual currency period, revaluation and devaluation – I had engineered it all. Now I was once again considering the idea of floating the currency – its first entry into an international market.

The kina had previously been tied to other currencies, a basket based on import-weighted currencies. Looking back now, because we were such a small little fly, we ought not to have put our currency on an international market and make it the subject of daily speculation. What we should have done, and should even do now, was just lock the kina to the US or Australian dollar and leave it there. But gradually our situation stabilised and we reopened trading, but we only allowed imports or any exportation of funds according to the revenue we had received. We had to go into strict monitoring and declarations by all the banks of their liquidity ratio every day.

Chris was a good Finance Minister. He was a smart cookie and he was the right person for the job. When he came in, of course, I was monitoring the whole thing and people would query me so much because I was the first Finance Minister and the longest-serving one. But there was a lot of consultation. Chris gained very good control of the situation. The measures we put in place went well and this gave us a little bit of time to do our homework and make sure that revenue was being collected. In order to do this more accurately I reorganised the entire revenue commission.

We used to have a Chief Collector of Taxes and then a separate Commissioner of Customs. I decided to put them both together.

I caused a reform in that sector and created the Commissioner General for Internal Revenue with a Commissioner for Taxation and a Commissioner for Customs, all under one. This enabled the government to monitor the revenue much faster than ever before. The first Commissioner General was Nagora Bogan, followed by David Sode. We were able to monitor the inflow of money and make sure that the Central Bank came into play, having a greater role in this process.

Sections of the export industry were put under the policy as they were collecting money that belonged to Papua New Guinea but were keeping it offshore. The mining companies, those big boys, were very powerful in themselves. They were playing the speculative game of earning high interest offshore and keeping their currency strong. They would say it was to pay off their debts and that sounded good, but it meant this money was not being counted in our reserve. I clawed them back in through our new measures.

The first three months in office were incredibly hectic and challenging. The IMF and the World Bank were also breathing down our neck and insisting what they always pushed for: devaluation. The World Bank's typical policy was that we should have what they called a Structural Adjustment Programme loan. In it they gave us 25 conditions we would have to adhere to, and required us to undergo an almost total reform of our financial system before they would lend us the money we needed. This went on for the next three years. They forced Papua New Guinea to take corrective action, which meant that when the Asian Financial Crisis happened, we were protected. A lot of the World Bank policies actually sent developing countries to the wall but, generally speaking, we were able to be selective in the way we implemented those 25 conditions.

When I came into power again, I also wanted to look at the possibility of reforming the provincial government system. Even at Independence, I was concerned that we did not have the capacity to run so many tiers of government or have enough properly trained people to work in it. Almost twenty years after Independence it was clear that the provincial government system needed reviewing. Whether the system was operating properly or not, we did not know. We had nothing to compare it with and there were few signposts for us to take as a measurement of how it was working.

There were very few people in the provinces sufficiently educated or trained to take charge of different portfolios, such as lands or public works. It was a completely different system from the traditional leadership that had existed for generations and the administrative system was a problem for people to grasp, especially in areas where the level of education was poor, or even non-existent. Those of us in Port Moresby, and in my case where I had been educated in Australia and trained as a public servant, were much better off. We'd had constant guidance from the colonial government and they had groomed us for the job. In the provinces the system of government had been run by expatriates, and there were few Papua New Guineans who had ever been exposed to this kind of administrative work.

The provincial government system had started to take effect in places like East New Britain and Manus and provinces close to the centre of government in Port Moresby and they had managed reasonably well. But in other provinces it was the traditional Big Man system that operated, where a leader came in to government to represent the people without knowing anything, except how to look after pigs, distribute land and pacify his wives. The issue of the mismanagement of the provincial governments had been brewing for some time, particularly when Paias Wingti had been Prime Minister and I was his deputy. We had set up the Law Reform Commission, headed by Ben Micah, I think in 1992, and given it a wide range of powers to look at the whole system and try to build into it a more responsible, decentralised form of government.

In 1983 the national government had already amended the law to make it easier for parliament to suspend provincial governments because there were so many problems. At a national level we patted ourselves on the back and said, 'Well, we are the only good government, the rest of them are not and we will just have to monitor them.' A lot of the provincial governments were subsequently suspended under the new law and so we had a government, now almost fully centralised, which started to be run by Port Moresby. We were regarded as superior and the national government as more important. That was the Big Man system and the national government was the biggest. We could say it was the re-centralisation of powers but we also made provisions to continue the decentralisation processes when the provinces were ready and more mature.

By late 1994 the plans for changing the system were still being discussed. However, there was a great deal of opposition from within the Papua New Guinea islands, which included New Ireland. Within days of my taking office, the island provinces said they planned to secede and create a Federated Melanesian Republic and demanded that they be given administrative control of their own affairs by early December. I am from New Ireland and I support greater autonomy – probably more now than ever before. As Prime Minister, however, I knew this issue would create instability and fragmentation of the country and with the Bougainville crisis ongoing, we could not afford more problems. I understood why they were doing this – the governments of the islands region had always been more sophisticated and economically productive and seemed to be better organised than many of the other provinces.

Some of the island leaders had been meeting in Rabaul around the time the volcano erupted and so, perhaps, there was some kind of Melanesian superstition at work – perhaps the leaders thought that the volcano destroying Rabaul was a sign they should not continue down the secession path. There was also the threat to arrest the leaders if they continued to meet.

Eventually, in June 1995, after a great deal of consultation and amendments, new legislation was passed for reform, to abolish the provincial government system and replace it with assemblies that would include people elected at a local government level.

CHAPTER 19

I had long held concerns about the general performance of the Papua New Guinea Defence Force.

The establishment of the Bougainville Transitional Government (BTG) took several months. There was enormous hope that this might begin to change the direction of affairs on Bougainville. There had been a lot of people, academics and lawyers, working on the framework of an alternative government to the old provincial structure. One of the advisors was an Australian academic, Tony Regan, who had been involved in Bougainville for a number of years. I thought he always put forward ideas that were concrete and very much taking the middle ground.

The transitional government came about in April 1995 after a series of meetings with Sam Kauona, Theodore Miriung and others at Mirigini House, the prime ministerial home. Miriung had been a magistrate and an Acting Judge of the High Court. He had given the Bougainville Revolutionary Army (BRA) legal advice so I understood he was BRA inclined, but he began to realise that there would be no end to the matter unless things changed. The fact that BRA leader Francis Ona had still not participated in any talks was not that much of a sticking point because he seemed to have been more or less isolated. We could not contact him but we had to proceed; we simply had to cut Ona off and keep the momentum going.

We dealt with Sam Kauona and perhaps during that time he became a little bit estranged from what was happening on Bougainville. I am not sure how much Kauona was relating the details of these meetings back to the BRA but it seemed to me that he may not have been that close. Other BRA members, like Chris Uma, were more directly involved in what was happening on the island and continued to be involved in confrontations with the PNGDF. Uma was a young militant on the ground leading the BRA group and was somebody we knew very little about. Kauona's position had changed, though. He had been a militant but now he was supposed to be in a more co-ordinating position.

I was prepared to go to a lot of effort to get the process moving and I spent some time travelling around Bougainville to do so. I was never concerned for my own safety because I always had a lot of policemen around and because I had had a long relationship with Bougainville due to the Coastal Shipping Company, going back to 1967. Although I may not have personally visited all the areas before, I happened to know a lot about the environment. My shipping company had been carrying the island's copra for many years and a lot of these people were long-standing clients. I had a familiarity with them and they had no reason to doubt me. Even though we may not have met, I recognised many names from the cheques that used to come in. One man I recall was John Kumkam, from an area close to Numa Numa on the east coast of Bougainville, an area that had been occupied by the Japanese during the war. I also knew the Chinese businessmen and many other people. I had an old schoolmate there too, Francis Seeto, who had been at Kekere plantation near Kieta.

It was not difficult to establish the BTG – it was a little like setting up the Gazelle Restoration Authority after the Rabaul eruptions. We knew we had to move on and it was a natural thing to do. The BTG was the bridge we created to cross over to a place where we could all meet. The role of the transitional government in my mind was to start to look at a new Bougainville. My attitude was: 'Let's think completely new and act new,' because what we had done in the past had not worked – not only had it not worked it had led to disaster. I was trying to inculcate in everyone's minds that we had an opportunity to rethink our approach and that we could, in fact, solve all these problems.

We began by granting a dispensation, an amnesty from prosecution, to all sides of the conflict. This was also an amnesty for those who had committed an offence against the state to be able to feel quite free that they would not be pursued. That, of course, was a tricky issue because of the Constitution. It was not clear whether the government would be able to unilaterally grant amnesty to a particular group of people without extending the same conditions to others. I made a Declaration of Amnesty and I suppose, looking back, we hoped that nobody would challenge it.

It was important that we restored confidence in the intentions of the Papua New Guinean government. The fact that I went to Arawa was a big turning point because I was quite well known to the people in Bougainville, in Arawa but also in Kieta, Buin and other places. I had also visited Torokina during my time as Prime Minister in 1980. In a sense my returning to Bougainville to attend the peace talks was just like coming home. Of course there was not a very big welcome because people were highly suspicious, but I certainly went there as their friend.

161

The BTG fared very well in the first few months. We continued the dialogue but we always encountered resistance. The BRA presented a strong opposition, even though it was an opportunity for them to express exactly what Bougainville wanted. It was Miriung who took a more conciliatory line but it was not an easy situation.

My understanding of why Bougainville had descended into such widespread civil war was that, once the BRA took the position that they were fighting for independence, anybody at all who did not speak for their cause was regarded as being suspect. The BRA went berserk. They were certainly organised in the fight for their rights, for their resources, against the mine and for independence. There was no doubt in their minds. They killed a lot of their own people who may have been pro-independence for Bougainville but had not openly expressed themselves or turned up to fight. This issue affected the people who had taken refuge in government care centres and were often regarded as pro-government but, for them, it really was just a question of survival. All of the people who came down to the refugee centres were considered suspects, and a lot of them were killed.

It is hard to define who the resistance fighters were and what they stood for. On the whole they were in the middle. They were resistant to the BRA and to the government forces at the same time. When the PNGDF was first deployed in the year the crisis began the soldiers were totally unprepared. They had not been properly trained for the kind of warfare or the type of security deployment that was needed on Bougainville. We should not have sent young people who knew very little about doctoring wounds in a community to try and resolve the issues as it only led to more confrontation. There was often talk about winning the hearts and minds of the Bougainville people through the work of the military but they were not up to it.

Another thing that is important to keep in mind was that we were sending, by comparison, light-skinned people who the Bougainvilleans called 'red skins' to go and fight the black skins. The people on Bougainville have probably the darkest skins in Papua New Guinea and a strong historical sense of their own rights – there may have been a long-standing resentment because of the domination of the white colonial powers. White skin was supreme for a long time and so the lighter pigmentation of the skin of the soldiers, the red skins, could have constituted part of the Bougainvilleans' resentment. They may have believed that it was the white men who had done everything in terms of taking whatever they had from them – their land, their resources – and therefore it was no different when the red-skin soldiers came, because they were going to do the same thing.

In 1995 I appointed Brigadier-General Jerry Singirok as the Commander of the PNGDF. I made that decision because it seemed to me that he was really smart and I was looking for an intelligent soldier to reorient the way the deployment was taking place. When I assumed office in 1994 I just inherited the army's existence on Bougainville – I was still not all that clear what they were doing there but whatever they were doing it was not working.

Part of the PNGDF's attitude on Bougainville was that they had gone in believing, 'We are the army, we have the rifles, we can put all this confrontation to rest, we can restore peace because we've got the military power to do it.' They repeatedly found out that it was not military power that would bring peace in Bougainville. They increased fear in a situation where the people already wanted to be separate from the rest of Papua New Guinea. When, as Prime Minister, Wingti talked about the conflict in terms of which side had the greater might, he was talking more about a traditional tribal environment, where the forceful military equivalent of the biggest tribal group has the power and can restore or even enforce peace. Bougainville was completely different and the purpose of the conflict was quite distinct from any other tribal conflict. In the Highlands region they might be fighting over a woman, firewood or pigs. These guys on Bougainville were fighting for their rights, their resources, their land and their freedom.

I asked Singirok to prepare me a thesis on how we should resolve the Bougainville situation and, being a man on the ground, he gave me his ideas on how to bring everything to a conclusion. His basic theory was that the military should be better organised, hit the target and restore peace. The root of his proposal was to eliminate the top command of the BRA and, once that was achieved, peace would be slowly brought back to the island. I am sure there were some sensible military personnel on the ground who just wanted the engagement to end – they wanted peace and were content with the strategy we were pursuing. However, there were also individuals who still held a belief that the only victory would be one of might – that the only way to victory in a Melanesian society was the elimination of those who were obstructing the process of peace. Elimination and might were probably ingrained in the minds of some.

Our soldiers were frequently caught in confrontations. Once, in 1994, during Operation High Speed, which Wingti initiated, the BRA had taken the high ground at Panguna and the PNGDF could not get out. Not only that, there were also problems in resupplying the forces who were running short of food. We had to fight our way out. That was why we asked the Australians to supply our forces with their helicopters, to assist us in getting out, but they were reluctant to continue their involvement in what they regarded as an internal conflict. They thought they had nothing to do with it although they were, in a way, very responsible for the confrontation in the first place.

I was disappointed because Australia had benefitted from the mine but were not prepared to carry the burden. To me it was quite suspicious that Australia would not wish to assist Papua New Guinea under the Defence Forces Co-operation Treaty. This was the time to provide help to bring peace to an independent nation, but for some reason known only to Australia, they withdrew. This was why, eventually, the question of another type of assistance was raised and that was where the existence of Sandline came into play.

Even though there was a ceasefire and we were making progress, there was still a central core of people in the BRA who had to be dealt with. I thought that if we used a strategy of arresting, demobilising or neutralising the leaders of the BRA and stopping their absolute resistance to authority, peace would then follow. We were not just dealing with people who only wanted compensation from the mine or independence for Bougainville – these were killers, murderers, and I'd had reports of many people being massacred. We were not dealing with sensible people anymore; these were people living out in the bush with cultish thinking. They were basically hard-core criminals, in my view, because they were disobeying the laws of the country, and somehow I felt I must put a stop to them.

In theory, of course, the amnesty extended to them and was an opportunity to bring everyone together so we could start talking peace. But there were groups that would not take part in any of the talks we tried to initiate. You could not reason or have any constructive dialogue with them; they simply refused us. I was constantly in contact with leaders like Sir Paul Lapun and John

Momis. I talked about the ongoing issues on Bougainville with everybody I could. I talked to as many countries as I possibly could about the situation, wishing that somehow they could provide us with the backing necessary to deal with a strategy of neutralising these killers who had remained unaccountable for so long. I did not really directly solicit them, as in asking them, 'Please come and help us,' because I was conscious that whatever they did would take time and time was of the essence.

The South Pacific Peacekeeping Force, which was deployed for the Arawa Peace Talks, had been a success story in itself, as it was the kind of force that influenced the psychology of the people, suggesting that the Pacific was united. Unfortunately, for a whole range of reasons, I had not been able to extend that operation to something more permanent on Bougainville and I had always been looking for a much longer-term solution for peace in the Pacific generally. My opinion was – and still is – that if we allowed smaller groups to play around and challenge the peace of any country we would have the possibility of instability and insecurity. I thought the bigger powers in the Pacific could invite smaller Pacific countries and their security personnel to get involved – the larger players were already spending money that could be used in other ways. We could operate in the South Pacific Forum in such a way that meant when we made a decision that a certain country in the region may have security problems or conflict, the South Pacific, as a group, could command this South Pacific Peacekeeping Force to act. The moment this was invoked, I believed, it would create sufficient psychological impact to neutralise any instability because the peacekeeping force would be big enough to deal with Fiji, Papua New Guinea and all the other little countries in the Pacific.

As we were a member of the South Pacific Forum, we were already doing joint military exercises. Australia was operating further afield as well, having joint exercises with countries like Singapore and Malaysia. I felt my theory was supported when we saw, with the loss of the Malaysia Airlines Flight 370 between Kuala Lumpur and Beijing in March 2014, how all the nations in the region with capacity to help joined in to search for the plane. Joint military exercises where different countries work together can be very effective.

Another instance that relates to this idea of a peacekeeping force was the establishment of the Regional Assistance Mission to the Solomon Islands (RAMSI) in 2003, when Australia led more than 2000 police and troops from all over the region to help establish better order after civil unrest had erupted. Australia had not wanted to go to the Solomon Islands alone because they were all white, therefore they wanted the Papua New Guinean blacks and countries like Fiji to join forces so it would be a multi-racial security force. Years after I had suggested it, Australia borrowed the very model I had proposed for Bougainville and did not appear to be as concerned as they had been back then about the cost. They did not call it a peacekeeping force, of course – Australia does not like to use that term. They used other language to try to avoid the connotation that there was trouble, but the forces would have shot if necessary to protect their lives so really they were there to restore peace. The wording was just a way of changing the definition a little. They went there to restore peace in the Solomon Islands and enforce the Constitution in a nation that was being destabilised.

The PNGDF launched Operation High Speed II in July 1996, because there was enormous frustration at the failure of the BRA to negotiate or to enter any discussions at all. High

Speed II was really a flow-on from High Speed I, which had fizzled out because the PNGDF did not back it up financially or militarily and this led to the disintegration of the whole exercise. The purpose of High Speed II was to try to contain the flow of equipment and arms coming from the Solomon Islands to Bougainville, to strengthen the border control.

Shortland Island was just a hop, step and a jump from southern Bougainville, near Buin, and there were a lot of incursions there. We tried to strengthen that border because of the inflow of foreign military arms, possibly directed by some of the Taiwanese loggers who were having dealings with Solomon Mamaloni, the Prime Minister of the Solomon Islands. Operation High Speed II was supposed to back up our capacity to ward off this infiltration. Kangu Beach, between Koromira and Buin, was supposed to be a very good passage. The PNGDF initially took control of Kangu Beach and were on the ground and in control. I believe the soldiers were listening to the Australian Rugby League and the BRA took advantage of that. They came and killed about six or seven soldiers and took five as hostages. The massacre was a fatal display of total ill-discipline and untrained defence force personnel.

The attack was really nasty; the soldiers were chopped up completely. You can just imagine when I heard that. My first question was: where was my Commander, Jerry Singirok? Apparently he was somewhere in Singapore. I immediately directed that he come back. He followed the instruction – if he had not come I would have got rid of him.

I had actually appointed Singirok on the basis that he wrote an impressive and thoughtful thesis on how to bring an end to the Bougainville situation. We were moving away from the direct on-the-ground simple battlefront strategy that had failed for so

While meeting foreign dignitaries was a professional highlight, nothing compared to reconnecting with the people of my birthplace on Tanga Island.

Receiving a warm welcome on a visit back to Tanga Island in the late 1970s. I spent a lot of time discussing community concerns and local politics with the people.

Indonesian President Suharto greeting me at the Asia–Pacific Economic Cooperation (APEC) meeting in Jakarta, 1995.

Having a laugh with Philippines President Fidel Ramos. Our two countries have long enjoyed a friendly political relationship.

Papua New Guinea has a privileged position as a member of the Commonwealth. I met British Prime Minister John Major in 1995.

I was raised a Catholic and educated by Marist brothers, so meeting Pope John Paul II was a special moment for me.

At the celebration of my 25th anniversary in politics, my father, Chin Pak, whispered to me that it was time to get out of the political game.

The national government in 1994, including Prime Minister Paias Wingti (third from right), Chris Haiveta (second from left) and Bill Skate (second from right).

Stella and I with our first grandchild, Cheron, Vanessa's one-month-old son, in 1993.

Paying tribute to my parents is an important ritual for me. I'm at my mother's grave in Rabaul with my brother Michael, wife Stella and son Byron.

The volcanic eruptions in 1994 destroyed Rabaul. It was one of the worst experiences of my life.
Image courtesy of AusAID via Wikimedia Commons.

Rabaul has since recovered and is as beautiful as ever, but the volcanoes could erupt again at any time.
Image courtesy of Lucy Palmer.

This little girl comes from remote Hela Province, where there is still limited access to healthcare and education.

The Mul-Baiyer tribe from Western Highlands Province is one of the many diverse cultures in PNG.

I feel very connected to Huris in New Ireland. It is a peaceful place and I spend time there whenever I can to relax and escape the pressures of political life.

All images on this page courtesy of Lucy Palmer.

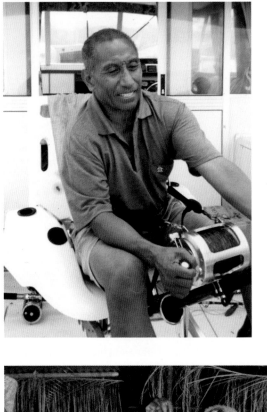

I am happiest when I'm near the sea. Here I am fishing for marlin off the coast of Huris.

As the Governor of New Ireland, I enjoy working at a grassroots level. In 2011 I went with the Australian Doctors International (ADI) team to Tanir. At the customary welcome, we received a feast with roasted pig. Image courtesy of ADI.

long. Brigadier-General Singirok had been injured in an earlier encounter on Bougainville and while I did not expect him to be directly on the ground, I certainly expected him to be in the country while High Speed II was taking place. After finding out that he was overseas, I began to question his ability to translate his thinking and his military training into an effective battlefront.

I was not entirely sure what Singirok was doing overseas at that time – it is possible he was meeting with Sandline or their rival, the arms supplier J and S Franklin. His only explanation was that he was with Defence Minister Mathias Ijape. Later Singirok was found to have secretly received thousands of kina from Franklin through a Visa account in London. The account had been used for cash advances, payment of hotel bills, airline tickets and clothing.

The Kangu Beach massacre was very bad. I do not know if the soldiers were drinking or otherwise, but an enemy is an enemy under any circumstances, whether you are sober or drunk. I was very disappointed with the performance of the PNGDF because we had a good chance to make an effective impact and the operation failed due to lack of direction and lack of discipline. It was another turning point in the history of the Bougainville conflict.

The next major turning point came in October 1996 when the leader of the BTG, Theodore Miriung, was assassinated at his home while he was having dinner with members of his family. His murder was a real blow to the peace process. The funeral was at Buka and I attended, without too many security people around me. There were a lot of rumours that the Miriung murder had been directed by the national government through the highest authority of the PNGDF. These rumours, of course, completely negated a lot of the processes of reconciliation and the arrangements we were going through at the time. There was never any implication I had personally directed anyone to kill Miriung. It was very clear that I was seeking peace and killing was not really my line of thinking at all.

I immediately organised an independent coroner from the Commonwealth Secretariat, a retired Sri Lankan judge, Justice Thirunavukkarasu Suntheralingam, and he concluded that Miriung was killed by members of the PNGDF as well as resistance fighters. None of their names were publicly released. Unfortunately, it seemed that in the eyes of our own soldiers and other government officers, Miriung had become an enemy. The payback system is the culture of the people in Papua New Guinea. It is deeply ingrained. The death of Miriung was the result of an upsurge of resentment that had built up on the side of the military. The coroner's conclusion was he was shot and the order came right from the top. It was never established that the orders came directly from Commander Jerry Singirok. Miriung's death was a great loss. I was really hard hit by it and when the inquiry pointed to the top man, that for me was the biggest wound in the whole process. I really wanted to get to the bottom of who killed Miriung but I never did manage to.

As a result of his work on the inquiry, the judge's life was in danger and he apparently received a lot of threats. He left the country on a Saturday afternoon just before his preliminary findings were made public. I do not believe that Miriung was generally regarded as a threat and I do not really understand the motivation to kill him. I thought that he was a frontrunner in the process that I was seeking to attain, whether he and I always agreed or not. I thought he was the connecting point between the government and the people in Bougainville but, as a result, he may not have been trusted by his own people.

The cost of Operation High Speed II, both in terms of lives lost and monetary terms, had been very high. We were to learn later that a lot of the funds released to help the soldiers and for restoration work in Bougainville had disappeared without explanation. It later emerged that a substantial amount was used to improve the PNGDF Commander's home, known as Flagstaff House, at Murray Barracks in Port Moresby.

I never did ask Singirok directly whether he was involved in the order to kill Miriung but there were plans for the Security Council to question him in March 1997 over a series of issues. We had been auditing the books of where the money allocated to the PNGDF had gone. The timing of this inquiry was at exactly the same time as Singirok made the decision to destabilise the government, so perhaps there were other motives at work.

Miriung's death had a huge impact on the process. It created a vacuum and all of a sudden everything came to a standstill. It seemed clear that it was time to replace talking with action.

Chapter 20

*I was in a position to try and resolve the
Bougainville crisis and therefore I had to do
everything within my power to achieve that goal.*

At this point we were heading towards the end of 1996 with no
solution in sight and the next national elections due in July 1997.
From the beginning of my second term in office I was committed
to resolving the crisis on Bougainville. I am not the kind of
person to take the chair and not resolve the main issue. I wanted
to bring this matter to a close before the election, not just for the
sake of politics, but so that I could pass the baton of peace to
my successor. Resolving Bougainville probably goes back to my
long-standing view that I had been given an opportunity so I had
to complete the task, we had to do it. I could not simply pass it on
for someone else to inherit the same problem. I wanted to win the
game and pass on the victory.

The origins of the idea of engaging foreign support and
advice over issues of internal security began long before Sandline
International arrived in Papua New Guinea in February 1997.
Defence Minister Mathias Ijape had been the Police Minister
under Rabbie Namaliu in the early 1990s and they had been

looking for some time into the possibility of creating a special force to take care of security at some of the country's mining operations, such as Mount Kare and Porgera. I believe there were plans to call it a Rapid Deployment Unit, and then later a Police Tactical Force, but neither of these proposals came to fruition. The idea of this emergency force was to have a unit that could deal quickly with law and order problems, particularly at the large mining sites – they needed to be protected because they were contributing so much to the national purse.

Ijape had already spoken to several forces, and I believe that was how Englishman Tim Spicer became involved. He had been a long-serving officer, a Lieutenant Colonel, in the British Army. He took a leaf from his own experiences and was involved in the establishment of a private military security force – I prefer that description to mercenaries, which has other connotations – known as Sandline International. The initial contact with Spicer and all subsequent contact with him and his associates was conducted by Ijape, Chris Haiveta and others. I first met Spicer in January 1997.

Shortly before this meeting I had travelled to the Marshall Islands to attend the funeral of Amata Kabua, who had been the country's first President and had served for seventeen years. I was the one giving a eulogy for him. I took *The Kumul* and was accompanied by Jerry Singirok and the Commissioner of Police, Bob Nenta. I wanted Singirok to come so we could really talk the whole thing through before we went ahead and appointed Sandline. Singirok was really pushing for it. He wanted me to consider a paper he had written as a submission for the National Executive Council. He also wanted to discuss the purchase of some Singaporean naval boats, so his planning was already well advanced.

I sat with Nenta on the way to the Marshall Islands. To get *The Kumul* there we went via the Solomon Islands and Nauru. On the way, I was talking to him about security because, if Sandline were to come in, they had to come under the authority of the police force and be engaged properly under the Constitution. If the Police Commissioner engaged them as one of the security forces, then they would act as police officers and possess the power to arrest people.

I talked to Nenta about all these issues and then on the way back I sat next to Singirok to talk about Sandline. He was very positive – there was never really anything said against the potential project. Singirok also talked about buying one or two of the Singaporean naval ships to give the PNGDF some greater border control between Papua New Guinea and the Solomon Islands. All the discussions we had were very serious and Singirok was really pushing me to immediately convene, as soon as we touched down, the National Executive Council (NEC) to consider his paper to invite in Sandline. I had planned to hold the first meeting of the NEC in mid-January, as they needed to be scheduled well in advance. Singirok wanted to bring it forward and call it an emergency meeting. I refused.

'No, I do not want any unplanned NEC meetings,' I told him. I felt I needed more time to really examine the ramifications of this proposal. First off, we needed to ensure that we had the money to pay for this operation and explore all the implications of such a decision.

The moment we touched down in Port Moresby I was whizzed off straight away by my security patrol because I was alerted to the possibility of being attacked in some way, possibly assassinated, or that perhaps the military people were going to do something to me. Nenta must have got the police to neutralise it because everything went smoothly. I never got to the bottom of what that incident was all about, but I would imagine it related to this group of people Singirok wanted in, and there may have been some dissension in the armed forces already.

I went straight to my parliamentary office where Ijape was waiting for me. I sat down with Ijape and he said, 'I have got Tim Spicer here, can I bring him in?' I did not know he was going to be there. Normally I would not entertain this kind of spontaneous meeting but I had already spoken to Nenta and Singirok and here was a person from the military firm that was going to be involved, and I did want to hear him out, however, I said, 'No, I'll see him later.' Before I see anybody, I always want to know their background and everything about them.

First, I went through the proposal with Ijape and he supported Sandline, just like Singirok, so they were working together. I told him to prepare a fuller brief and reiterated that we had to make sure we had all the financial information we needed. This was very important because the country was going through a pretty lean time. Anything that I spent on this type of expenditure would affect the process of restoring the economy. Chris Haiveta was not involved in the discussions at this point but I asked him to give me an independent assessment on the financial implications. I did not know the exact price at this time but I had a fair idea of what it would be. That was also another reason I did not want a sudden meeting with Spicer within the next 24 hours. I wanted all the information to come in first.

Ijape was trying to persuade me to hold a special meeting to approve this as soon as possible but I did not wish to. However, I liked the idea that he proposed to me. It was through our discussions that I realised how long this idea had been floating around. This was a scenario that Ijape had been painting for a long time – it was originally supposed to involve the police, but now it seemed the idea would suit the Sandline proposal. Ijape had everything planned because they had already been meeting with the people who ran Executive Outcomes, a private military deployment company which had worked with Sandline on projects in Africa, and also with Spicer. On their side it was conclusive. On my side, it was something I still had to consider.

After meeting with Ijape, I decided to meet with Spicer and my first impressions of him were good. He knew exactly what he was talking about and he was really talking my language. I was money conscious, of course, and aware of the fact that there had to be a timeframe to this exercise. Spicer was special, very impressive. He was truly British and he was just brilliant. He was plausible and, being a very disciplined person, he heard me clearly. Militarily speaking, it was also terrific to listen to someone of Spicer's calibre with precise ideas and the ability to present them clearly. When we talked about firepower he had all the details ready. He was already engaged in another military exercise in Africa and had years of experience in the British Army. He was a professional man and his background spoke for itself.

Soon after, I told him, 'If we go ahead with this, your position will be right next to me in my office. You will be taking command from me because I need someone who will listen to me.' I told him what I had told Ted Diro back in 1980 when we were sending our soldiers to deal with the secessionist crisis in Vanuatu: I did not want anybody to be killed and if it was not possible to guarantee that then I wanted minimum casualties on both sides. I told Spicer, 'You are not allowed to kill any of my citizens. Although you may be within the operation, you will only fire in self-defence. You are here to train, to help, to fly aircraft and have use of this equipment but not to shoot.' They were very clear instructions.

I shared my thinking with him about how the whole strategy had to have a psychological component so that we could show hard-core Bougainvilleans who were resisting peace – and I was trying to use a Melanesian way of thinking here – that they would know the government meant business and that we had the power to knock them out if necessary. I knew we still needed to have the firepower but I was going to use psychological warfare in terms of a superior militia. I thought we could use firepower to show them how powerful Papua New Guinea was by just annihilating a village up there at Panguna, such as Guava, which was where Ona was presumed to be. A lot of people did not realise that, concomitant with all this, I was planning to borrow a leaf from America in the Second World War.

Shortly before dropping two atomic bombs on Japan in 1945, the US government had dropped over five million leaflets in Japanese on the cities of Nagasaki and Hiroshima, warning civilians of the impending attack and telling them to evacuate. I was going to do the same. I thought we could co-ordinate a massive release of information to tell the people to get out. I would have people on the ground to lead the villagers out and we would then blow up the target without anyone there. The long-term strategy, once that show of power had been made, was to restore peace. I felt this action would be enough to convince the hard-core fighters that the game was over.

Ordinary Bougainvilleans, generally from the way I have understood them, were really quite practical people. I felt I knew them. But it was their leaders who had talked out of bounds, creating supernatural scenarios, opening up a new window of thinking to the Bougainvillean people and filling their heads with the idea that they could be living in a paradise because they had the natural wealth in the form of gold and copper in the mine. I used to dream at night, and often I could not sleep wondering, how we were going to put an end to this crisis. My mind was working almost 24 hours a day because this was so crucial, I had to do it, without losing too many lives, and I had to succeed.

I did not worry about how bringing in a foreign force might be perceived. I was not looking at it as a foreign force, but more a powerful force. Singirok and others had already met with Spicer, his superior and the chairman and everybody in Sandline well before I had direct contact. The possibility of restoring the copper mine at Panguna was never really a consideration for me, it was the furthest thing from my mind – I just wanted to stop the unnecessary killing and massive expenditure. It was not raised as a possible benefit.

It would have been good, of course, for the mine to be operational but I did not go there. If I could convert Bougainville into productive expenditure instead of just consumption, I would have been very happy but the reopening of the mine was secondary. I did not get pressured on this issue and, in my mind, if I could bring peace the mine would probably automatically be able to reopen at some point.

The contract to engage Sandline was presented to the National Security Council to make the initial decision. The proposal was then presented to Cabinet, but we wanted to keep the details absolutely confidential. Chris Haiveta, as Finance Minister, was in charge of the funding issues – whether we would have to borrow money and whether we could repay the money without exposing Papua New Guinea's borrowing or debt.

The Security Council approved the proposed Project Contravene on 15 January 1997 and the final contract – with the operation now called Project Oyster – was signed at the end of January at a cost of US$36 million. When I approved the deal I did not have any understanding of how Haiveta had been involved in private discussions with Sandline for reasons of his own. It was also not until several months later and the events of 17 March that I began to have a clearer understanding of Haiveta's direct involvement with Singirok on this matter.

At the time Haiveta was on a mission to launch Oregon Minerals, which was the business investment arm of the government in mineral projects. Oregon was not supposed to be involved in the funding of the Sandline contract – it was a completely separate thing altogether. We were able to fund the project because we had restructured our whole internal revenue flow. I was very, very confident at the time that we would have quite a big surplus. I did not think that the cost of the contract was a lot, because I was looking at our progressive monthly revenue and we were already exceeding what had been budgeted. Not only that, the ongoing costs of Bougainville were over $100 million a year. I was able to look at the Sandline proposal as a special case, and a decision was taken that we would still be able to balance the budget.

My understanding, in terms of the contract, was that Sandline was going to come into Papua New Guinea and bring in their expertise and training and work alongside our PNGDF. According to the information I got from their submission, they had previous experience in Africa, in Sierra Leone, and had done a pretty good job. At no time did I ever regard them as a mercenary force. I believed that Australia had been in that game during the Vietnam War, and around that time the Americans were also engaging military firms to do a lot of their security work, so I saw no real issue with getting some of this experience

179

from military firms. Based on the outline given to me, I was convinced that we could do it but we needed Sandline to come in and train our PNGDF first. Later, there was a feud between Singirok and Spicer because I think they were starting to talk about who was going to control the operation. There was no doubt in my mind that the Sandline soldiers would be under the control of the PNG government.

It never occurred to me that it might create a problem to bring foreign military personnel into Papua New Guinea – I never looked at it that way and probably misjudged the whole thing. I was probably more ruled by passion and the desire to bring the whole Bougainville dispute to a conclusion and I underestimated the controversy this would create. I was more morally concerned than politically concerned. I had to bring the matter to a close. It had been inherited by Michael Somare, by Rabbie Namaliu, by Paias Wingti, and now it was on my table. The crisis had been very damaging to Papua New Guinea's international reputation and I had worked very hard to try to mend our image – I even went to the United Nations and talked with the UN Special Advisory Department and did a lot of work on this behind the scenes.

Sandline was going to come in for only a short period and I was prepared to ride it. Another aspect of the operation that appealed to me was that some of their soldiers were African, they were dark-skinned – these were not just white people coming in.

The contract was signed and the first payment was sent off. I was not overly concerned about the confidentiality of the contract. I knew that the details would eventually get out and, for me, when I calculated it, it was well within our capability. Once the contract was signed Sandline personnel started to come into Papua New Guinea within days, although I never met any of them myself. I had met Spicer's associate, Michael Grunberg – he was more a financial expert for Sandline. We did not talk very much but he was satisfied we had the money to finance the project. I was more concerned with strategy and I was confident in my discussions with Spicer on that subject.

Chapter 21

I am sure Australia played a big role in influencing the media war over the hiring of Sandline. That was the war I was not ready for.

The story of the Sandline contract was revealed in the media in early February. I presumed that while we were having talks with Tim Spicer that the Australian government would have known what was happening as they had intelligence people in Papua New Guinea. However, as far as I was concerned, and perhaps I was sometimes naive in a sense, I thought Australia would not interfere in an independent country's decision-making.

The story was leaked and from that day on, from that moment, the media never stopped. The media were not necessarily collaborating but it was a very accomplished distribution of the kind of information that Australia wanted to be made public so that it could destabilise the situation and force the removal of the Sandline forces. Having Sandline personnel in Papua New Guinea was not in Australia's interests and, in my subsequent meetings with the Australian hierarchy and Prime Minister John Howard, I became convinced that there was a lot more to their opposition than what was apparent.

Howard was very, very much against the situation but I just could not see what Australia's real interest in wanting to stop it actually was. I could not lock their interest onto any particular thing. Instead of talking about the number of people who were being killed, that Bougainville as a society and an economy had gone to the wall, they were just talking about getting rid of Sandline.

When the story initially broke I did not feel it was too damaging. I thought that, generally speaking, Bougainvilleans were beginning to welcome what we were doing because, as soon as it became known that we were going to send in these special forces, the flow of people to the government care centres began to increase. I am pretty certain to this day that if I had been allowed to do it, I would have got Bougainville under control. Most of the people I talked to supported it. The people who sent in communications were not politicians but from the general public, people within Papua New Guinea, people from Brisbane and some of my schoolmates. I do not think they could see anything wrong with what we were doing.

All the governments around us were quiet on the matter, all except Australia. Without Australia, perhaps we could have got the support of even the Association of Southeast Asian Nations, ASEAN, but not one of them said anything. I did not hear anything from Suharto, the President of Indonesia; nothing from Lee Kuan Yew in Singapore; and very little from the United States. I heard from a few do-gooders in New Zealand who wanted to bring peace but, except for them, I cannot recall the NZ government opposing it very strongly.

I was not ready for the onslaught from the media. I was completely caught out. I did not have a media unit to be able to retaliate, to put the message across. The Australian media kept pouring out stories day after day, they were just extraordinary; there was a war on me. One of the most influential voices from the Australian media was Ray Martin from Channel Nine. He came in very hard again and again. These opinions were repeated by our own media. I would not have minded if they had come openly to debate the issue with me but they did not. They just played on people's psychology in making them feel negative about the exercise, but who among our people would have been able to say that Sandline's involvement was not good? The kids on the streets who took part in the demonstrations, how would they know? They were just incited by the media. This was not the kind of war I could compete with. It was the battle over the people's minds and I was losing – the people were convinced.

I attended a private lunch with Prime Minister John Howard at Kirribilli House in Sydney shortly after the engagement of Sandline was revealed. I spent four and a half hours alone with him on a Sunday. His attitude was: 'Just get rid of these people. They should not be there.' He did not give me any good reason for it. I told Howard to stay out of the affair, mind his own business and not to interfere with the decision of my government.

'We are an independent country,' I said. 'We play by the rules and the rules are that you are not to interfere with a sovereign government, and this is a decision made by Papua New Guinea as an independent nation.'

I was able to talk like that because it was just Howard and me and I was able to tackle him on his own ground and simply state my case. He got the message very clearly. I do not think that Howard has ever liked me since. We left that meeting with an old saying – we agreed to disagree. Ultimately, there was something missing for me in the whole nature of my conversations with

Howard and other Australian officials. I simply thought that there was no good reason for Australia to object to this deal. To me, it just did not add up, even to this day.

It could have been that Australia's attitude in this matter was linked to an interest in not wanting to see foreign influences in Papua New Guinea other than themselves. We were now dealing with people who were bringing in the kind of armoury that Papua New Guineans had never had before. Australia was possibly worried that this could create an atmosphere of misconfidence, especially as we share a border with Indonesia. Perhaps they were concerned that all of a sudden we might think that we had the firepower to deal with the illegal border crossings on our western side. Perhaps Australia did not want the possibility of a war with Indonesia. However, Howard gave me no reasons, he simply threatened Papua New Guinea, that if we continued, then there were agreements he could terminate. He suggested that I think about it.

'I'll send an envoy to come up and talk to you,' he said.

It was too much. I suppose if I had been a little bit more political than principled it may have been a different game. I was the Prime Minister and, having made a decision, I took absolute responsibility to fight for it.

Howard sent up special envoys, all of whom had had long-standing dealings with Papua New Guinea and included very senior diplomats and defence advisors: Hugh White from the Department of Defence, Allan Taylor from the Department of the Prime Minister and Cabinet, and Phillip Flood from the Department of Foreign Affairs and Trade. I almost told the envoys to get out. They raised the possibility of increasing their assistance under the PNG-Australia Defence Co-operation Program if the Sandline personnel were kicked out. I was also threatened that if we did not do as they wanted, certain aid agreements could be affected.

'It is your money and your decision,' I said. 'Beggars cannot be choosers.' I was prepared to stand my ground. Of course, I would never want to engage in a big fight with Australia but I would not allow another country to interfere in our decision-making process. They never made good on their threat – they did not have to because they succeeded in stopping Sandline anyway.

On 16 March 1997 I had been in the Southern Highlands Province visiting the Governor, Dick Mune. We had been talking about various resource projects in his province and had stayed for a night at Ambua Lodge just outside Tari, looking at birds of paradise. The next day, St Patrick's Day, Stella and I flew back to Port Moresby on *The Kumul* and Singirok made his announcement on the radio that the Sandline contract had been abandoned. Apparently the National Broadcasting Corporation had been intimidated by soldiers and Singirok had made a statement on Radio Kalang. Singirok had accused me, Defence Minister Mathias Ijape, and Deputy Prime Minister Chris Haiveta of corruption and demanded our resignation within 48 hours. The night before, all the Sandline personnel had been arrested under Singirok's orders in an event that became known as 'Operation Rausim Kwik' – Pidgin for 'get rid of them quickly'. The news of Singirok's announcement had broken in Port Moresby but I knew nothing about it even though several of my staff were urgently trying to contact me. It was Peter Niesi, the journalist, who broke the news to me at the airport.

I had no warning at all. My immediate reaction was that Singirok was committing treason, that he should be put in jail. My other conclusion was that he took this action to divert attention away from his own actions, his possible involvement in the murder of Theodore Miriung and the misappropriation of money meant for Operation High Speed II. Prior to his announcement, the last time Singirok and I had got together it was very cordial, especially when he was pleading for me to think about the second-hand naval ships from Singapore. That was his deal, but I did not like the thought of second-hand military equipment. However, I did not know about his deals in London with J and S Franklin, a weapons manufacturer and distributor, or his extensive contact with other executives from Sandline International – nor did I know that Franklin and Sandline were effectively rivals. I understood that Sandline did not require any equipment because they already had enough from their own previous operations. They were planning on bringing this equipment into Papua New Guinea, which really annulled any commitment Singirok might have already made with Franklin.

I was very disappointed that Singirok, the man who got me to cross the river, was the person now opposing the very thing he proposed to me. Although Singirok was talking about corrupt activities on the radio, I do not think any suggestion of corruption was ever directed at me as such. If there was corruption, and it emerged later that there was, then he would have known about it because of his own dealings. Nor was I immediately concerned about the conduct of my two ministers Ijape and Haiveta. Having said that, at some stage it went through my mind that it was possible things I did not know anything about could have been privately arranged by these two ministers of the crown.

In a way I was shocked but my greater reaction was to feel somewhat depressed and disappointed. It was no less a situation than the Last Supper, when Jesus had Judas at his side and then got sold the next day for those lousy 30 pieces of silver. I could not imagine that a military person in a democratic country would attempt such a thing. They were supposed to be men

187

of honour. Singirok was now entering a completely different arena – politics – and I was not going to allow this. The PNGDF was supposed to protect the Constitution of this country, not to violate it by making demands and entering into a political sphere for its Commander's personal ploy.

After I landed, I went straight to my office. I did not need to think for very long – Singirok could no longer be trusted. By midday that day I'd made the decision to sack him as Commander of the PNGDF and appointed Colonel Fred Aikung as Acting Commander in his place. All the Sandline equipment was removed to Australia but the difficulties with the military continued. Several problems arose at Murray Barracks between different groups of soldiers and the crowds that had gathered outside the barracks. Extra police units were called in. The protests on the streets continued and there was some looting of shops near the barracks too.

PNGDF Major Walter Enuma, another key player working with Singirok, had organised the operation to kidnap and hold the Sandline personnel. This action was totally illegal. I intended to make sure that Singirok suffered the consequences, but in the meantime the Sandline men were under the guard of the military so I expected the military to resolve it. It was in their interest not to prolong the confusion by holding on to these people for too long. I thought it was best if they released the Sandline soldiers as quickly as possible, and they eventually did.

The protests, which got larger with every day, caused business and normal activities to come to almost a complete halt in Port Moresby. There were continuing tensions between the army and the police. I had no reason to think that the police force was anything but loyal to the government at that point. They were the superior element of security.

With the situation continuing to worsen, the Sandline deal was cancelled and I announced a Commission of Inquiry. However, Singirok and Enuma continued to demand that I, and the ministers involved, resign. Even though I had sacked Singirok and appointed Colonel Aikung, the military have their own ways of resolving internal issues and so we had to allow them to do it militarily – they have their own codes of conduct and disciplinary measures. Whether they allowed Singirok to stay in the PNGDF or go was really a matter for the new Commander. Colonel Aikung had been recommended to me by the Security Council – I had never met him before. Unfortunately, Aikung was attacked soon after his appointment. Soldiers burned his car and he was forced to go into hiding. Singirok would not move and continued to stay in Flagstaff House.

Clearly this matter was not going to be resolved quickly or easily. I was certainly concerned that we had this ongoing deadlock and the potential for further problems. I was never really concerned for myself; I knew what my job was. It was to ensure there would be no contravention of the Constitution and to deal with the consequences of law and order emerging from that.

The next session of parliament was due on 25 March. As the date drew near, crowds of people began to gather outside the parliamentary gates, including quite a large number of uniformed PNGDF soldiers. I had no qualms. It was up to me to prove to the nation that there was no corruption on my part or anybody I knew within my government. I had gone through this before. I was prepared to open up the books.

Before the parliamentary sitting I had a meeting with Walter Enuma. He never actually demanded anything – like a good soldier, the moment he meets a superior he immediately salutes and keeps quiet. However, his presence was sufficient to mellow me.

I could have taken a confrontational approach but I did not. I put on my thinking cap and gave more thoughtful consideration to the consequences, and this approach somehow subdued the tension with Enuma and the one or two other people who had come with him. Enuma was, more or less, the leader of the group, the Rausim Kwik operation. I listened to them. At the end of our discussions, because of the manner in which Enuma and his men presented themselves, I thought the heat of the crisis was over and it was time for me to restore the integrity of parliament, and ensure the protection of the Constitution. I got notice that the parliament was beginning and I was going to allow the issue to be debated, and so we went in.

I was a bit late so I rang up the leader of Government Business, Andrew Baing, and delayed the sitting a little. When I came in there were two sides in parliament. Veterans like Sir Peter Lus spoke very strongly against the involvement of the PNGDF in politics and the question of the delicacy of them infringing on the Constitution. There were also two sides in my Cabinet – there was a group who were pro-military intervention, who I called the hawks, and then the others, who I called the doves, who were more timid in their approach.

I was not prepared to resign that day. I would never step down under that kind of threat. Never. That would have set a very dangerous precedent in PNG politics and sent us towards anarchy. We had worked long and hard to establish the country as a democratic society where the rule of law was paramount – giving in to these kinds of demands would have been a disaster not just at that time but for years to come.

Whenever there has been a crisis in Papua New Guinea, it is just like the crest of a big, big wave that could destroy everything in its path. But somehow, like a wave, the crisis lands on the shore and recedes. I thought by this point, we had gone past the crest of the wave, the heat of the dispute, and people were starting to view the situation with cooler heads. Now I had to restore confidence in the government of Papua New Guinea. I was also making up my mind during the course of that debate, after meeting with the soldiers, after listening to the pros and cons, knowing that at some point I had to step aside. I entertained the vote calling me to resign.

The motion was moved by the leader of the Opposition, Bill Skate. I loathed Skate because I could never trust him. I shared a lot of confidential information with him – he had been very well briefed personally on this in full and absolute confidence by me as Prime Minister. He had come to see me with another member and I told them everything about the engagement of Sandline, about our capacity to pay, about the revenue flow, and that it was my idea to bring all this to a close before the election. When he moved that motion for me to resign, it was a stupid step.

If I had resigned, there would not have been a government because my deputy was also being asked to step aside. We would have been in chaos because, under the *Prime Ministerial Act*, if I was not there the deputy would take over. But I went through the correct parliamentary democratic system by allowing the debate to proceed. I won the vote, probably two to one. Handsomely, you might say. A lot of the members abstained from voting. But I had won and there was nothing my opponents could do. However, outside parliament we still had a problem with the crowds, which included members of the PNGDF.

In terms of security, all the police guns were pointing at the military people. One word from me and they would have gone off. However, I decided that life was too precious, that I should not – for the sake of my position – put the whole nation at risk.

The crowds were yelling and shouting and throwing rocks but the police said nothing. They were very focussed, very well trained, very loyal, and I take my hat off to them. The PNGDF would have completely scattered had I gone through with it. The police were well prepared, they had the escape route set. There is no point in me talking about it now, but I went out through the back door. On the other side, they had the police car, fully armed, waiting for me.

That was probably the most confronting experience I had ever had as Prime Minister. That night was unpredictable, as the protesters had effectively laid siege to Parliament House and many people were unable to leave. The following day, I was determined to get the House to decide on the fate of Papua New Guinea. That morning I had gone to Boroko Police Station and I went to parliament with the Deputy Police Commissioner in his car. I was surprised that the police had such foresight – they seemed to know exactly what they were doing and I do not think I could have had any better security.

The attitude of the police towards the PNGDF at that point was that they were going to protect the government of the day. The police were still alert and well positioned. Some of their top marksmen were strategically located on top of the hill near parliament, watching every soldier to see if they tried to stop cars or interfere with the democratic process.

The Deputy Police Commissioner was determined we were not going to stop for anybody, but one of the soldiers managed to stop the car. The Deputy Commissioner opened the front window and showed the soldier his rank. I sat in the back with two police officers with machine guns waiting to see what would happen – if the soldier had acted we could have been killed. I could have never imagined a scene like this in Papua New Guinea.

The Deputy Commissioner had a pistol and he simply said, 'Hey soldier, I am going in.' The soldier did not react, and so we drove into parliament.

Chapter 22

I had to go on, I had to rise from the ashes, just like Rabaul.

Foremost in my mind that day was to restore tranquillity in the nation. Parliament had reinstated confidence in me as Prime Minister and now it was left for me to decide. I did not want the instability to continue and I wanted to conclude this chapter as quickly as possible. Following the conciliatory approach from the PNGDF and the victory with the parliamentary vote, I was on top of the world. Having won all this, I wondered, what should be my next step?

I wanted to allow the proper processes to explore whatever suspicions existed. I announced that I would step down and also said that I would remove two ministers, Chris Haiveta and Mathias Ijape. I appointed John Giheno as Acting Prime Minister for the duration of the Commission of Inquiry into the Sandline deal. If I had been looking to simply protect myself I would have appointed my deputy, Albert Kipalan, who was also the deputy leader of the PPP. However, I wanted this whole process to be impartial and John Giheno had a reasonably good name. He was from the Pangu Party, and a solid person, so I appointed him to maintain neutrality throughout the whole inquiry.

I'd had a lot of really loyal staff and ministers around me during my term as Prime Minister, people like Warren Dutton. They were not only loyal to me, but faithful to upholding the Constitution of this country, and they would not have given one inch to anyone who tried to interfere with it.

Not long after I stood down, the Commission of Inquiry, chaired by Australian judge Warwick Andrews, began. One of the issues explored by it was whether there had been any corruption involved in the Sandline contract. I subsequently learned from the inquiry that Chris Haiveta and Mathias Ijape had gone to Hong Kong to meet with Michael Grunberg and other members of Sandline and its associated company Executive Outcomes, and that US$500,000 had been cashed by the company. Judge Andrews later went to Hong Kong but could not verify any recipients. I did not even know that the ministers had gone overseas.

Some years later, I went to England to have a chat with John O'Reilly from Lihir Gold, and I also made a very special request to meet up with Grunberg. This is totally unknown to anybody, until now. Grunberg took me out to dinner. The only question I put to him was: 'Can you tell me who got the money?' I thought it would put my mind to rest to know.

'It was revealed in the Sandline Inquiry,' I told him. 'You can just tell me to satisfy me. Who actually got the money?'

Being a trained military man he simply said, 'There are some things we can neither confirm nor deny. We do not talk about such things.'

I came to my own conclusion but it would be for others to make up their minds about what happened. During the inquiry I also learned about the role of Nick Violaris, who was supposed to be the coordinator of the PPP. He also went on the trip to Hong Kong. Nick did not have direct access to me all the time because that was the way I ran the government; he was dealing more with Chris Haiveta. Nick was also a successful businessman in his own right. I had known his father, a highly respectable person, and we had got along pretty well. But Nick let me down completely – he ran away from the Sandline Inquiry, he just disappeared. He tried to make contact again in the lead-up to the 1997 national election, but I refused to see him. That was it, finished.

I told the Commission of Inquiry – and the second Sandline Commission of Inquiry held in August 1997 – the facts as far as I knew them about the hiring of Sandline. My lawyer told me there was nothing that implicated me but there could be some dark patches here and there. The wrongdoings did surface – Singirok had accepted money from Franklin and he had lied to the inquiry. After the second inquiry Singirok was charged with sedition, although these charges were eventually dropped. However, the findings never concerned me nor implicated anybody in particular with real proof.

Once the conclusions of the first Commission of Inquiry were released, I was not going to prolong the situation of waiting to resume office. I had held an inquiry, it was a public inquiry, there was no proof. I was not going to allow one more minute to pass for anyone else to continue to persuade the nation that there was any evidence of corruption. As soon as Singirok's involvement was proven, I was not going to play marbles with him anymore and nor was I prepared to prolong my re-entry into parliament because there were now other forces at play.

Giheno, who I'd thought was a strong man, was somehow being influenced by others who had political motives to keep me out. Some fingers pointed at Rabbie Namaliu, who was the Speaker of the National Parliament and had been a member of the original Gang of Four. Maybe Tony Siaguru from Transparency International was involved and definitely Meg Taylor, now the Secretary General to the Pacific Islands Forum. All these goody-goody people got together and tried to prolong the whole affair. When I heard all these things were happening, I decided to resume the prime ministership in early June.

'I am taking over. You can now move out from my office,' I said.

Ahead of the July 1997 elections I was really well received by my people. But the fellow who stood against me for the seat of Namatanai Open, my traditional cousin Ephraim Apelis, was standing for the National Alliance, Michael Somare's party. He was from my area and was the Administrator of New Ireland, so he knew from the 1992 election returns where I had got all my votes. I lost the election by 110 votes but I discovered that over 1500 votes were missing. The system let me down – somehow the areas in which I got all my votes people's names happened to not be on the Common Roll, they had simply been removed. Elderly people who had voted for me for almost twenty years found that all of a sudden their names had disappeared. Subsequently the case went to the Court of Disputed Returns. The judge accepted that the people were not on the electoral roll; however, he said it was not within the scope of his inquiry to address the issue.

The loss of that election was very depressing for me. Of course, the Sandline business had been damaging and the PNGDF were also trying to run me down. We also had Somare and the National Alliance, and they wanted to come in with a bigger number of votes, and Somare was no new boy to this kind of game. He would betray any agreements with me for political convenience. One could say I had a lot of enemies.

When I got the results I was at my home in Huris. I just could not believe it. I became very, very disappointed and depressed. I was the first Prime Minister since Independence to lose his seat. It was a significant experience. My staff found it harder to accept but one thing that kept me going was the thought, 'Well, that's life – that is what it is all about.' I just told my staff to co-operate and make it happen, to make it the best transition ever.

This was the worst thing, politically, that had ever happened to me. In business there had been times of hardship and financial difficulty but these were nothing like losing an election. However, the greatest thing about it all was that I was cleared of all the sins of which I was accused. I gradually accepted the verdict and went about my life. The thing that would have hurt me most was if I had been convicted of corruption.

My father would have been very happy. He had always wanted me to go back to where I came from, to the world of business. However, it was not long before I faced another crisis. Every time I became somebody in government my business went down. I had sold my shares in Coastal Shipping when I became Prime Minister and later I had to divorce myself from my aviation company. When the volcano erupted in Rabaul, we had tried to keep the airline running and relocate the 160 staff. We decided the best way to do this was to take over Nationair, which was owned by four Papua New Guinean pilots and had a big hangar in Port Moresby and a small fleet of King Air aircraft. I was really compelled to take over Nationair because my aviation business in Rabaul had no home. I had to come in and compete with Airlink and even half of Dennis Buchanan's business, Talair – he was fading a bit by this time. It was very difficult, shifting the base, shifting the company, and competing with well-established operators. When we moved to Port Moresby our expenses went sky high, because it was really expensive compared to Rabaul, and so we made the decision to borrow foreign currency. Shortly after the 1997 elections, with Bill Skate at the helm, the kina collapsed. What I had borrowed doubled. I had to find ways of negotiating the repayment of those debts and the interest was pretty high.

It was a very difficult time. We had to sell the aircraft in a really tough market – some in a fire sale, some went to Brazil, and we ended up mostly with just helicopters. I tried to impound some of the aircraft we'd sold because the buyers were not making their monthly payments on time, but the legal costs were heavy. The courts ruled in their favour, saying that although they were late they had not said they would not pay. Because I could not enforce these payments some people walked away, having just paid the deposit and a couple of instalments.

I had a lot of debts and I had to go and meet the lender and bankers and negotiate a settlement. All I was fighting for was to stop the axe coming down on me because I owed too much. That was when I really learned about the world of banks. Although I had created the banking system in Papua New Guinea, I did not know the foreign attitude of banking – they were very firm and I had to find a way to reach a resolution with them. I was able to do that, to deal with all the lenders so that they could accept the settlement amount and not the outstanding loan. It took me eight years to finally walk away debt free.

Looking back, I somehow think even with the misfortune of losing the 1997 election, I was lucky to be able to spend my time outside politics and sort out these issues. The problems in Papua New Guinea really began when Skate became Prime Minister that year. He wanted things done and he forced people to do what he wanted. He took the lyrics of the Frank Sinatra song

'I did it my way' and followed them. Public servants either did what he wanted or they got the bullet. That was the beginning of the public service finding loopholes to do things that were not normally done in order to meet directives and keep their jobs.

Skate did not last. He was a very poor Prime Minister for the country. He just did not know how to govern and he also ridiculed himself, creating a lot of international disrespect for the status of the Prime Minister of Papua New Guinea. He did a lot of damage politically in the minds of people who were concerned about proper governance but others just treated him as a cowboy. He would get excited and would take over the microphone and sing in nightclubs and start dancing. The general leadership took a different course when Skate took over. Where they should have been concentrating more on the policies of building a nation and reviewing their platforms, they began to concentrate on other areas to build up their personal wealth. When money came into play, greed soon followed. The politics of money began to take over and many people contributed to it.

A new breed of people came into the government after the 1997 elections. Every time a politician opened up his mouth he related the policy to money and money became the prime attraction in elections. That was never the case before. We had talked about hard work, we had talked about policy and about incentives to build a better society. Now it is different. There is not one statement that I hear anybody say these days which is not related to money. Looking back at the statements the PPP made, it was never about money. We never talked about wealth being the most satisfying thing in life.

This reverts back to the typical system of the Big Man in Papua New Guinea, his grip on wealth, having possession of more wives, more land, more pigs. This is how people still think of leadership.

Now we are talking about notes and coins instead of land and pigs – they have become the same thing and I do not know when we are going to get out of this way of thinking. Corruption is not purely about money. Corruption can be defined in many ways and has many forms. If you get paid and you do not do any work, you are corrupt. If you are a lazy worker who does not fulfil the terms of your agreement, you are corrupt. If you do a deal without even having the money and there is a conflict of interest, you are corrupt. Corruption has become so widespread now and it breeds at the highest level where the Big Men in government make a deal. Then the people start thinking, 'If it can be done at that level, then when it comes to my area of responsibility, I should have a bit of it too.' It flows from the top right down.

Unfortunately now it is entrenched right throughout the system – both in private enterprise and in government services. It has become a question of, 'How much will I get for doing this?' It is very, very bad and it costs a lot, not just in monetary terms but also by delaying the system, holding it back, not allowing projects to take place, and retarding the process of reaching conclusions. That is another area that is costing our country dearly; it's the biggest problem we have in Papua New Guinea today.

Chapter 23

I am a Governor now. I think that I am doing much more as a Governor than I was doing as Prime Minister.

After losing the election and being cleared by the inquiry, I had a clear conscience. I could look people straight in the eye and the whole community never looked at me as though I was somebody who just came out of a prison, an ex-convict of some kind. In a way, I was quite personally satisfied inside. That feeling of certain dignity and respect was continued by the population. However, there was remorse back home – they wanted me to continue to participate in politics but I distanced myself.

In 2002 I allowed Byron, my son, to stand for the Namatanai Open seat and he won. I had not stood for the seat so that he would have a chance. I was very happy he won the election and the victory restored my status. The people just swung to him even though he was not that well known in that area. I went regional and competed against the then Governor Ian Ling-Stuckey. I did not campaign as strongly as perhaps I should because I was relying on the Namatanai votes to get me in. However, I did not judge Ling-Stuckey's penetration in the Namatanai area as well, so he had the upper hand. I failed to return to parliament and to full-time political life but I was not in the wilderness. I was very busy. Politically I was not able to be as influential as I had been but that did not bother me.

In Australia when you are out of office you are out. In Papua New Guinea, even when you are out of office, you are still a public figure; you still have to deal with the people. I'd had previous experience of being out of government after I left Michael Somare in 1978 and at this time I was busy enough worrying about my own business, and so I just got on with that.

As I've said, I had sold my shares in Coastal Shipping to pay for the children's education, and my brother Michael subsequently also sold out. He had engaged himself in real estate but after the Rabaul volcanic eruption in 1994 he went right under and his wife had to go through dialysis treatment in Australia. He was now in dire need of something to do. He is an active person with a good shipping background and so, although I was not altogether au fait with the way they were operating Coastal Shipping, I thought maybe I could go back into that line of business again, make it successful and help Michael at the same time. So we started Vanmak Toby Limited – it stands for Vanessa, Mark, Toea and Byron.

Michael runs it; I do not interfere. He looks after all the management and I have engaged a Filipino accountant to assist me, to make sure that when I want the accounts they turn up. We have still not discharged all the assets I have in Islands Nationair – we are just slowly selling out. I also have some units in Port Moresby that I got Mark and Toea to run but they belong to the new breed of people and I would say 20 per cent of their time is used up by their families. They earn good pay – all of them get better pay than my salary as a politician.

I have always enjoyed good health – apart from my heart problems – and now as I grow older I pay a lot of attention to my diet. I always eat noni fruit before breakfast, I am careful about what I eat and I exercise every day. I even gave up smoking. In about 1979, after I had left the Somare government, I was a frequent smoker. Smoking was a way of relaxing, feeling sophisticated. I used to smoke, blow it out slowly and suck it back in through my nose. I was a big head then. One day, as I was leaving the house, I saw I had enough cigarettes to last a few hours. I looked at that packet and I said to myself, 'After this one I will not smoke anymore.' But as I was driving out through the gate I thought, 'Why do I wait until I have finished this whole packet? Why do I have to wait until after this one? If it is not good, if it is going to kill me, then I should stop.'

In that moment, that was that, I just made up my mind. That was the end of it. Partly it was my conscience at play but it was also the influence of my heart problems. So I decided that smoking was bad for me, that I had to give it away. I gave the driver the packet, threw my lit cigarette out, and that was it. For twenty years I had been smoking and I just gave it away.

The same thing happened with alcohol. I was a good drinker, not a heavy drinker. I did get drunk sometimes, but not too often. When I did get really drunk I would get so intoxicated that I would have to vomit. I've had that experience probably several times in my life. It was a horrible feeling. I would start worrying, after a drinking session, whether my heart was going to stop beating. I loved my drinking and during the second term of my prime ministership, I introduced wine into the parliament. Wine was a sophisticated drink then, as Papua New Guineans did not drink it; most people did not even know it existed. I used to know the labels of the wines and which was the best one and I got used to it. Whisky and ginger – they were my favourite, especially when it came to Johnnie Walker Black Label and Blue Label, they were the top.

When some of the ministers who had a problem wanted to see me, I would say, 'Well, let's have lunch and talk it over.' After one or two glasses of wine, the ministers would sometimes forget what they really wanted to talk to me about or, if they did manage to get over the effects of the wine, it would just soften the tone of their purpose. I found that this type of consultation, sharing this element of casualness and drinking with the boys, was a nice way to lift frustration, dilute the tension and improve the relationship.

It was probably in about 2000 or so that I decided I wanted to test my willpower. Could I say no to having a drink? I thought if I could do without the prime ministership and survive it, then I could also do without drinking. Actually it was a self-test, to see whether I had the power to decide what I wanted to do and do it. Out of that thought process, I just decided to give up, and I did. It was not hard. It helped that I could reflect on the time when I had my last cigarette and so I could say to myself, 'Yes, I can do it.' It was a test of my willpower and reaffirmed that I could control myself.

As a result of giving up alcohol I felt a lot better. I could work longer hours and I could think more clearly. I sometimes wondered whether I should take it up again – it was not as if drinking wine was forbidden in one of the commandments. In the weeks that followed my decision, however, I felt more alive. I had also been aware that I sometimes had symptoms of gout after drinking wine and pains in my joints. All these things helped to consolidate my decision and my commitment to good health. Even though I have grown older since giving up wine, I have found that I am able to work harder than ever before.

It never really occurred to me that I might have been much more effective as a Prime Minister if I had not been drinking at all. If I had to do certain things like drink wine in order to conquer, then I would consider that a way of life and that it was not necessarily a bad thing. If I had been too rigid without drink, I would not have had the kind of government I had and there may have been a negative outcome. However, it is hard to say how different it might have been. I do not think you should ever go back and deal too much with the past because it would tell a wrong story.

As the 2007 elections approached I was determined to prove that I could win the regional seat, particularly because of the earlier discrepancies on the electoral roll. After a visit to my banker, however, I did not think I had the resources to fight Ling-Stuckey, who was already a minister and had been the Governor of New Ireland since 2002. Paul Tohian, the former Police Minister who had been Governor from 1997 to 2002, had stepped down – he subsequently died in 2004. Ling-Stuckey had too many resources. His ability to mount a very good campaign was partly as a result of what I had done for him years earlier. He was one of the businessmen who controlled the poker machine industry in Papua New Guinea and that licence was given to him during my reign as Prime Minister. The fellow who helped him to get it was Ben Micah, who he then kicked out at the election. Ling-Stuckey had enough resources to knock anybody out of the game.

Contesting that regional seat was difficult. Ling-Stuckey had the resources to take thousands of people to his islands and accommodate them. He held meetings and totally indoctrinated these people. There were a lot of stories about the way he operated. However, this time I was more strategic. My campaign was carried out a lot better than it had been five years before. I defeated him by about 2000 votes and became Governor of New Ireland.

It is very rare for anybody to make a comeback after ten years in limbo. You do not see too much of that. I was supposed to be gone, but I am still here. I did not feel as if it was a great thing that I had been restored to a leadership position. It was not something new to me as I had been there before, higher than that. The position of power had never really meant anything to me. As Prime Minister I had been focussed on building a nation, a unified country that would be able to stand up alongside all the nations in the world. As a Governor, I began to touch the lives of individual people.

I had never concentrated on education but now I have focussed myself very strongly on ensuring free education. I have introduced a whole new range of initiatives so we now have an old age pension and a pension for the disabled in our community. We have introduced a series of human, imaginative policies that make life a lot better and fairer for everybody. My role now is to lead the people from their neglected way of life to a more promising future.

In my first hundred days of office I did not hesitate at all. I called in international experts and top officials to a one-week seminar in Kavieng. Out of that we ended up with over 159 resolutions and then I asked them to narrow it down – they ended up with 39. Even that was too big so with a few of my friends we made it even more concise and ended up with a document called the Malangan Declaration. I am very determined to transform New Ireland according to the vision of that declaration, which focusses on the development of business, infrastructure, social justice and better service delivery.

In terms of my role, my function in national politics is virtually nil. The only national function I perform is to attend the National Parliament when it sits. The role of Governor has been much harder than that of Prime Minister. I am constantly on the ground and dealing with a lot of people's problems rather than policy issues. I visit the villages, the wards, and then the councils and there are nine councils in my area. I have to deal with the presidents of those councils and try to make them work, to lead them by example and to encourage them to follow. The provincial government system still does not have a very good reputation in Papua New Guinea but I have set a strict timetable so that we meet up every three months, four times a year. If we have special issues to deal with, we call extra meetings and we run on New Ireland time – which is on time.

The state of the public service in New Ireland when I became Governor was totally invisible, non-existent, undisciplined, and very corrupt with people on the payroll for not working or working on the sidelines. They did not know what they were supposed to have been doing and that situation was not really their making. The system was created by my predecessor, Ian Ling-Stuckey, who established what was known as an illegal Limus structure.

Limus was the name of the island that Ling-Stuckey came from. After he was elected in 2002 he used his political campaign co-ordinators to conduct service delivery in their local government areas and paid them for this work. Under that structure he directed that all the powers under sections for requisition by the government be transferred to his personal staff and he ran the whole of New Ireland his own way. Ling-Stuckey practically took away the whole administrative structure, the whole legal structure, and replaced it with his own. That was why there was really no trace of the kind of projects he had spent public monies on. All I can say is that he spent almost K12 million a year from the royalty money from Lihir. During his term of office this resulted in over K60 million of untraceable public money.

When I took over the government I walked into an empty space. There were no records, no nothing. All decisions made by the provincial government – and I imagine most of these were illegal without a proper Cabinet or even enough members for a quorum – had been made by one man. There were documents of concern from the Ombudsman Commission directing Ling-Stuckey to retract the direction of taking over the power of the Administrator but that was, just like everything else, forgotten.

We had information and an audit but the kind of evidence required to successfully prosecute was non-existent because even the computer was totally stripped. Only Ling-Stuckey knows who he gave everything to. You could find the cheque going out, but it went out to a company, a supermarket or to people who were acting as agents of the government to buy books even though they might have been engineers or carpenters. I had expected problems when I came in but there was absolutely no guide. No decisions had been recorded for the previous five years. I do not think that the Cabinet Secretary had recorded anything by the look of it.

All Ling-Stuckey's personal staff – and there were hundreds of them – of course, they just disappeared. We really had to start rebuilding the Provincial Administration from scratch and training people to do their jobs.

'We can turn the ship around,' I told my supporters before the election. 'But the crew of this New Ireland ship, they are not going to be easy to turn around because they are human beings. It will probably take five to ten years before we successfully reorientate these people to think like government servants because they have been totally out in the desert.'

I had a lot of consultations with those who were prepared to listen to me – at that time a lot of people had been bought. Many of them sided with Ling-Stuckey and they were very unco-operative. It was difficult to get them together because Ling-Stuckey had never attended to the Administration at all, so they were totally dislocated. I started by just visiting the office regularly and telling people to be on time.

Those offices were so filthy we had to clean them up. They were an eyesore. People had not been turning up for work on time and some of them were having a big holiday and we did not know where they were. The people at the top did not know where the public servants had gone – some had gone off to do other work and were still on full pay, and others stayed in their offices. Some of them were already retired or had been retrenched but were still staying in the government houses and refusing to leave. It really was a nightmare. The place was in total chaos. I worked very long hours but, because this was at a grassroots level, you could actually see the transformation of your words into action on the ground.

With one stroke of the pen I was able to reverse the ratio of recurrent to development expenditure and that was one of the first things I did. I knew it was not going to be easy but it was a demand I made because I wanted to put more money into development so we could move forward. We had to have 70 per cent for development expenditure and 30 per cent going to the public service in recurrent spending. There had been a total imbalance and distribution of funds because of the way the Ling-Stuckey government operated. His perception of government was completely different to mine. Under his model, the government was there to hand out lollies all the time and keep everybody happy. After years of this behaviour, it really has been difficult to get the people to fall back into a normal way of life.

It worked this way partly because of the traditions in Papua New Guinea; it was really handed down by our culture. The Big Man always made the feast and started the distribution of resources for debts, for weddings, for birthdays, for a church opening, for any extraordinary days he wanted to celebrate. People depended on the Big Man to provide, to make decisions, to direct the sharing of the resources so they have grown up with that expectation, that mentality – it is not necessarily a failing of the system. However, these days it is money and consumer items instead of the distribution of traditional wealth or food. People now gather for a feast and they take home saucepans, primers, pressure lamps, blankets, teapots and buckets. In some cases it might also be dinghies and cars. This issue is right around Papua New Guinea but under the previous government of Ling-Stuckey it had been comprehensively organised as a way of securing continuing support.

When I became Governor I could see that all the roads, all the infrastructure, almost everything I had helped build in my time as Member for Namatanai were gone to pieces. My predecessor made comments about how roads did not vote for him, schools did not vote for him, it was the people who voted for him so they deserved saucepans. So the roads were run down, all the infrastructure was completely run down, the hospital had no medicine, the place was in total despair. Now we are reopening and maintaining those roads. There were also 24 rural aid posts that had closed down and so apart from maintaining and resuscitating the existing ones, we are also building new ones.

We have spent a lot of time restarting stalled projects and fixing broken infrastructure as well as dealing with the fact that the people had been taken away from a responsible approach to life to being completely dependent on the giver. We set out to promote the idea that those who will work will reap the fruits of their sweat, which was why we created the Sweat-Equity Grant – for those who planted new plantations of cocoa and copra the government would give them a one-off grant of K2500. Before this people had been going to work and instead of being hands on, they had their hands out.

My hope is that we will lead the way to becoming the model province of Papua New Guinea. New Ireland, whether I say it or not, is the ultimate spot for tourism. When people have exhausted the world, they must come to New Ireland. The province has all the elements to attract different kinds of people, including those who might want to watch sharks. Shark calling is a tradition in New Ireland that a lot of people around the world are interested in.

The sharks come out when the fish, the little *talai*, which are like whitebait, are at play. Shark calling is actually fishing because the local men like to catch the sharks. They rattle coconut shells near the canoe as if the fish were fighting and the sharks come. Another way locals catch sharks is to hang a noose with rattling shells and the shark comes up through the noose. A rope attached to the noose is connected to a wooden propeller, which is spun round to tighten the noose and the shark will be drowned and float. And that is how they traditionally catch sharks on the west coast. It is probably the only place in the world that does this.

At a certain time of the year when sharks are plentiful the men go out in canoes and they go through customary preparation. They fast and must follow other restrictions before they go out. All these things are hidden. They do not tell us very much about it. I have caught big sharks behind my boat but I have never dared to sit in a canoe and catch one!

CHAPTER 24

I think life is a series of events and you have to face the tide and the winds; you go out into the world and you try and conquer.

Papua New Guinea has changed a great deal since Independence, particularly in the last decade, and with the resources boom and new technology the changes are coming fast. We are still trying to get communities motivated to expand above a simple lifestyle and some areas are more productive and harder working than others. We are building a lot of real business people and they are in control of quite huge operations. A lot of this innovation, surprisingly, seems to be coming from the Highlands. They seem to be a hard-working core of very determined people who want to create wealth for themselves. This does not surprise me in one sense because, when I'd visited the Highlands – for example, when I went to see where Iambakey Okuk had come from – I could clearly see just how people had to work to survive, let alone be successful. They had that work ethic because they had to struggle to survive whereas for people in the coastal areas, life is much easier, there is more space and food is more plentiful. That is why there are more millionaires up in the Highlands, from sheer hard work, although they are probably 80 years behind the coast in terms of exposure and contact with the rest of the world.

The Highlands is quite disadvantaged in many ways because you do not have easy access to infrastructure and transportation. The ruggedness of the land has very much affected the rate of development in that part of the country because you cannot easily expand or build roads. The engineering costs would be too great and the remoteness of so many villages will remain so for some time to come. The people up in the Highlands are very determined and they like to make things work. They talk a lot, they emphasise what they want people to believe and then somehow convince them to make certain decisions. They are very much people on the alert and wherever they go they are protective because that is the way of life up there. People from the islands do not live like that. We do not even know who is behind us. If someone was behind me I would not even notice but Highlanders are very security conscious.

You could say that Highlanders are quite a driving force in Papua New Guinea's future but they are also a terrible force in Port Moresby. It is negative in the sense that they are squatting; they do not have jobs. Food is the most important ingredient of survival so Highlanders have been squatting on people's land and establishing gardens where they can; over time they have pushed the traditional owners, the Papuans, out. Now the whole of Port Moresby is like that. The Papuans are almost back into the villages and the whole city of Port Moresby and its surroundings have been taken over by this more forceful group of people.

The Highlanders are driving the buses and the taxis; they are running a lot of businesses in the city. That is the way it is now because of the kind of lifestyle back home in the Highlands and the difficulties of survival there. Port Moresby is a paradise for them.

The Papuans are very nice people, they are not at all aggressive, and so that is a problem for them. There are also now a lot of intermarriages taking place and life is going on. The Papuans will not know anything until all of a sudden they will realise that they have got no more land to build a house on and that is when the trouble will begin. It will happen – we have not seen the end of it yet.

Mobile phone technology has had a huge impact on the country. All communication, including radio, is very, very important. The new digital communication networks allow people to connect with friends and family all over the country and to access a great deal of information about what is happening not only at home but also in the world beyond. It is another path to development. It is bringing efficiency into the whole system and enables the young people to stay far away from their families but keep in touch. It is no longer just a question of getting up in the morning, looking out to the horizon and seeing a bird of paradise and the waterfalls anymore. People are well informed about things they would have known little about twenty years ago.

In terms of the future of Papua New Guinea as a whole we can go two ways. One is where we will be stronger, more united and successful, or we are going to be completely shattered. You just have to look at all these countries like Russia, where from one large nation they became so many splintered regions, and the problems that came from that have still not been resolved. Therefore the Papua New Guinean government needs to be very sensitive in the way they apply policies. They need to pursue one policy of uniting the country all the time and transcending fairness to all, especially with greater recognition of the smaller groups of people. We are going to need a lot of goodwill to be able to do that. We are fortunate that the people of PNG have patience, resilience and acceptance. Behind everything is the strength of our culture and the diversity of the country.

For the next twenty years or so we have enough resources to be confident but the more critical question is whether we are running the government properly to be able to attract the people to develop them properly. Minerals and other resources are really the most important thing in developing Papua New Guinea.

I am getting a little bit worried about PNG becoming over-wealthy or over-developing because we could end up similar to the Dutch. Economists often talk about the Dutch Disease in the economy, where there is a significant increase in the exploitation of natural resources and a decline in agriculture or more traditional sources of revenue. If this happens, we will lose touch with the real world of long-term survival.

In terms of the question of whether Bougainville will opt for independence from Papua New Guinea, this will be the sentiment in a lot of other regions if we do not nurse it properly. On the mainland it is not going to be easy. There will be a lot of confrontation and this by itself will promote divisions. The people who are able to easily cut the rope from the rest of the country are the island people. Bougainvilleans are safe; they are far away from everybody. East and West New Britain are a little bit different but the geography of the island is sufficiently divided for East New Britain to be able to take control. I suspect that in the next fifteen to twenty years, after another three elections, we will see how this nation unfolds.

We have got to see who is going to lead in the next round, and the next round and the next. They will be educated and they will be completely different from our contemporaries now – they will be more sophisticated and able to judge the best opportunities to take the country forward.

There are a lot of very short-term decisions being made that have nothing to do with where Papua New Guinea will be in another 100 to 200 years. People talk about development being based on high-rise buildings, Mercedes cars or Range Rovers. The mentality is still confined to this Big Man system, which is a culture in itself.

I am not sure I am optimistic about the country's future, I am a little bit uncertain. We really need very dedicated people, people who will abnegate their self-interest for the good of the community and they are not very easy to find these days.

Something that characterised the early days of Independence was the mentality. It was not wealth, it was commitment to the cause of self-government and independence, everything that would lead to prosperity and build a more satisfying life. Even the idea of prosperity was not foremost – adequacy, self-reliance, those were the words we used. We were more interested in the fair distribution of wealth.

In Papua New Guinea, development is much harder because of our geography. It is one of the roughest countries on this planet. Due to the remoteness and also the diversity of culture, languages and traditions, it is very, very difficult. If, overnight, we all become something like a robot, like a drone that just engineers itself and forgets about the human ways of thinking and judging things, then there would be a great future for Papua New Guinea. On the other hand they always say diversity is the greatest strength of unity. Perhaps what they really mean is that because we are so different, we cannot come together, and in the olden days the tribes with the biggest numbers would always win. That regional grouping is happening. There is no doubt that the Highlanders are becoming dominant, especially in government. There are now more than three million Highlanders in a total population of over seven million. Under the democratic system we have inherited, the regional grouping that has the greatest numbers will emerge as the controlling body.

In 2008 Joseph Kabui, a leading secessionist and the first President of the Autonomous Region of Bougainville, came to Kavieng to reconcile with me, the Governor of New Ireland, and to carry out an exchange of traditional gifts. Due to the massive publicity against me over Sandline, he said he wanted to put the matter in perspective, that he had no grudge against me. It was a big gathering in Kavieng and we both planted trees as a sign of peace and our growing relationship.

After he died, I went to Bougainville to reciprocate the reconciliation and it was a great success. This was a typical way of approaching things in PNG and I had no qualms about it. I thought it was something that needed to be done, as it was clear that many Bougainvilleans had totally misunderstood what I had tried to do in 1997 by bringing in outside support.

A date has yet to be set for a referendum on the future of Bougainville and right now they have enough fish, cocoa and copra to survive. However, if they do not have a mine they cannot be self-reliant, they cannot sustain any real development into the future. If Bougainville does become independent then I think the other island provinces will want to follow, including New Ireland, and I would support that.

If Bougainvilleans declare themselves independent then, by virtue of their status, they will be forced to think of things that will sustain them. In time, the leaders who oppose the reopening of the Panguna mine, the Chris Umas, the Sam Kauonas and all those people, they will not be around. Even if they are around, they will be too old to be active and therefore they will be overtaken by the younger generation. Unfortunately for Bougainville, because of the years of neglect and confrontation, the generation that is maturing now have lost years of education so it will be a longer process.

We need not only committed leaders who are dedicated, honest, and fair – the virtues of those things must really come into play. When we began in government we had a common purpose – to rule in order to develop the infrastructure and education for the good of our people. That vision has been lost. People continue to talk about it but there is no feeling behind their words. It is only said or done because of the need to cultivate more support – it is not done because of the genuine desire to do things for the good of tomorrow. Unless we have a real common purpose in life that all leaders follow, those succeeding will simply continue on the same path we have now. If everyone points to the same direction then we can have a great future. Short of that, it is very precarious.

We really need angels to guide us. For a country of mostly Christian people we pray hard enough. In almost everything we do we pray to our creator, even to make sure that the food is purified before we eat it. I just hope that the way we think and make our decisions will also be purified, and it will not just be a case of our prayers going nowhere.

CHAPTER 25

The gap between rich and poor that we are always talking about in Papua New Guinea is continuing to expand.

From the beginning of my political career, I have always believed that ownership of resources should remain in the hands of the customary landowners. My emphasis is really a belief that the people should have their rights protected and they should be able to exercise any negotiations themselves. It was not for a government to unilaterally just do it by virtue of an act, such as the *Mining Act 1992* that declared almost all the rights of everything to the state.

Another consideration should be how does a government stop landowners from making decisions that may not be in their best interests? That is what governments should do. We need strong guidelines to make sure that whatever happens it should not go beyond an acceptable point for continued exploration or development of a mine. We should be able to set the parameters in which negotiations can take place.

These guidelines should be equated with more developed countries that have already been in this game for a long time. We should look at Peru, Norway, the United States and African countries like South Africa and Zimbabwe to investigate the benefit of sharing arrangements they have in place. If Norway considers 51 per cent equity to be reasonable, then maybe we should have something similar, although not unnecessarily so huge that it prevents an incentive for people to invest. If we see that America has charged 12 per cent royalty, then surely we could consider increasing from 2 to 10 per cent and still be in the range of the developed and developing countries.

We do have a lot of examples of developing countries that have imposed the kind of benefit sharing for their resources. Papua New Guinea has chosen to do it in a particular way, which has really meant that we have undersold a lot of our resources. The reason I am pushing more for this now is that I have seen that things have come to a point where, after so many years of Independence, the opportunities are really only being given to those people who are already pretty well off, who are educated. I see one way of curtailing that lopsided division overnight which would be to transfer the resources back to the people. The next question might be, 'What if people just spend their money on cars and drinks?' For me, it is up to them because if the money comes to the government in Port Moresby it is misappropriated and corruptly abused anyway. Why not give it to the people? More importantly than that, I believe in the economic philosophy that the wealth of the nation must be in the hands of the people. Once the people are well off, they have greater capacity and self-reliance. Over the years the state has taken all and given back nothing and that is why villages remain in the backwaters – even though they are rich in gold, they continue to stay as they were because the money never comes back to them.

I am not suggesting for a moment that the benefits of resource development should go only into the landowners' pockets, far from it. They should also go to the provinces where they could

221

be used to develop infrastructure, the schools, the hospitals – all those things. The national government, the people, the provincial government, the local government, each should have a share and each should carry its own responsibilities. At the same time, put the capacity and the wealth in the hands of the people so that they do not have to come and beg their government to do things for them. This is an important ingredient, to translate our philosophy on self-reliance by giving the people the capacity to do things.

I have learned a great deal through some of my observations of China over the years as well. When the nation was rich – or at least the people at the top were – nothing actually happened in the country as a whole. There was a lot of corruption from Chairman Mao right up to Deng Xiaoping. When Deng Xiaoping took over he started to liberalise ownership of the land a little bit and then China started to build up. The situation of 'one for all and all for one' just did not work. If you work ten hours and you get ten kina and those who do not work still get ten kina, no one will want to work, there is no personal incentive. Under the development strategy that Deng Xiaoping introduced in China, the transformation started to take place. It took them almost 35 years to turn China from what it was to what it is today.

One of the big issues in terms of negotiating mining leases or any kind of exploration licences is the difficulty in identifying who the landowners are. Those issues still exist even if the government is in charge, which is why we have continuous sabotage. Even now, on Lihir, the landowners have wrapped a *gorgor* leaf on the gate of the mine to stop the mining pit from making any more extractions. The *gorgor* leaf, which is just like pyrethrum and comes from a ginger root plant, is a symbol that the landowners want to negotiate and has been widely used for generations in

New Ireland. When someone puts a *gorgor* up that means there is a dispute and that people need to sit down and talk. It is a very nice, non-violent way of telling people there is a grievance.

In Papua New Guinea, because so much of the land is customarily owned, there are often disputes or competing claims, particularly where there are benefits to be gained, for example, in a mining lease. There are problems when the companies involved do not engage in adequate initial preparation and work out the whole genealogy of the clans. In the old days, when the Australians were still here, they had the Commissioner for Land Titles and before they gave any land titles to anybody the Commissioner would go in and map out the whole genealogy of the clan so there would be no dispute. It would all be recorded and when the land was declared to belong to a particular group and was given out, it stayed as it was.

Some of the mining companies that go into an area and try to establish genealogy these days are cowboys. They just go in, find an influential group, then that group sets out the borders of their land and that is it. That is why we have disputes because it was wrong from the start. There will be a clan but there may also be sub-clans so, even if the mining company or logging company can identify the main landowners, they may not know all the politics of that group, the history or the disputes that may already exist over a certain parcel of land. It is very complicated and even if the government came in and said, 'That is state land now,' it would not solve anything. That is why we will always have land disputes because customary ownership can be very complex.

In Papua New Guinea land is life, it is as simple as that. It is not just a piece of dirt. You can see it in New Ireland – coconut and *taun* bananas, food everywhere. In Papua New Guinea, and probably other parts of the world, it is the same: what people do not see, they do not need. They have survived thousands and thousands of years without and it is only when people start to introduce consumer items that it triggers people to want things.

Nokon, of course, is very special to me. It was my mother's place, although her clan was not originally from there. They survived on all the *kapiak* (breadfruit) trees, the coconut, the fruit, and all the shellfish in the reefs. Nokon is everything, it is heaven on earth to the people there, and Nokon, to us, is just like that. It is the paradise we know and the root of all our survival comes from there. All of a sudden if we did not have aeroplanes, the truth is we could live without them. In the village, we have always gone without such things and we can live from the land, and from the sea around us.

Papua New Guineans have been very privileged in many ways because even if they have gone to the town or the city they have often had a place back in the village they could call home. Sooner or later this will not be the case and they won't have anywhere to go because land is getting scarce. I think ten to twenty years from now it will not be the same. People will have to find somewhere else to live because there is competition back at home, even among clans.

I have seen many cases where people have been absent from their customary land for a long time but they are still recognised because of the strong kinship and clan system. By tradition they are always recognised but these customs are changing. The logging and mining industries have taken the land where the people used to grow their food and it is shocking to see the damage that has been done to the soil. It is amazing to see a place like Ok Tedi or Porgera, where they graded all the mountains and chopped down all the trees. And what is it for? It all ended up in a gold bar. After all this, it is totally unrelated to daily life. The fruit trees are now gone. How can you explain this to the people, when they have been eating fruit from those trees for generations and now they've been chopped down?

For some Papua New Guineans, they have also had their family graves uprooted, completely desecrated. This has had a great detrimental impact on all their ancestral beliefs, their forebears. When you see the damage the resource companies do, it is not easy to understand. All the chopping down of trees, and the aeroplanes and noise pollution just end up in that little shed, no bigger than a room, full of gold bars. The people in the villages, they have no value for the gold. They know, of course, that if you sell it you can get money but you cannot bite it, you cannot eat it, you cannot share it, and all the trees and the whole environment are gone. When you take that into consideration, in terms of the lives of the people in those areas, it is not easy to accept.

In an ideal world that money would have been distributed for roads, schools, hospitals and other infrastructure. People would have seen some tangible benefit. In so many places they have not seen that so it is very hard to explain the benefits of a system like mining, very difficult. I am often very upset because of the destruction caused by logging companies. Situations like that have come about because a company has been granted a licence through the national government. I, even as Governor of New Ireland Province, do not have enough say in what is happening. That is because someone in Port Moresby is getting paid, greased. They have just signed a piece of paper, got paid in most cases, and they have left the problem for the people on the ground to sort it out and live with the burdens it creates.

That is just greed and, of course, many of the people making money in Papua New Guinea now live in a completely urban environment. They have cars that require fuel, and they have houses that require money to pay for the light bills and the telephones they use. It is the pressure of city life that completely erodes their passion and their understanding of life in the village. If anything happened to the village it does not affect those people at all.

On Lihir there are a lot of company personnel coming onto the island, over 3000 of them. Once they've extracted all the gold, all these big boys will just simply move on. They will leave their gadgets and equipment and everything there. The whole place will be left with all the mess. No one will ever look back to the people and say, 'How are they going to survive without the gold mine?' Not one of those expatriates is going to stay in Lihir – they will just walk away from Newcrest to another mining company in America or elsewhere. It makes it even worse for so many of the young people who have grown up on Lihir during the life of this mine. They have never engaged in agriculture, not even in planting potatoes and yams. They do not even know which season is which or when it is time to plant or harvest because they have been eating bread and butter and consuming food that has been bought in a store. They haven't got a clue on how to plant *kaukau* (food) or a yam or a taro.

When the Lihir gold mine shuts down it is going to be complete hell for the people there. Whenever I have talked about ownership of the land, I have always had in mind that I want the people affected by these large developments to be able to build up that wealth for the life after the mines. It is going to be a sad, sad story for all these young kids who have now grown up on Lihir. I have wished sometimes that we did not find Lihir because for us it has really meant very little. Investors have got billions and billions out of Lihir; we have got peanuts. And yet our day of reckoning is yet to come.

Bougainville is an indicator of how things can go, even Misima. The gold and silver mine on Misima Island in Milne Bay closed in 2004 and everybody just walked away from it and left nothing, not even a road. Lihir still does not even have a ring road around the island after years of operation.

We have to change the law. We have to start again.

CHAPTER 26

Since Independence, Papua New Guinea's most significant relationship has naturally been with Australia.

There has been a significant shift in the years since Independence in the calibre of Australians who really know and understand Papua New Guinea, people who have had a long and close involvement. There are different kinds of Australians now in Papua New Guinea and there are individuals who are very good, some of the most dedicated and genuine people you will ever come across. How I can describe Australians to be such is because I had a friend in the late Ken Tresize. I cannot think of anyone who dedicated his life so much as Ken did for the good of my country.

Australians are very down-to-earth people. I believe that because some of those people in the colonial era were bosses in my country and yet years afterwards I was able to find them driving taxis in Australia. For them, it did not matter, they were still working and they were proud of both worlds. Those are the kinds of people who have elevated the stature of Australia. A man might have been a Kiap in Papua New Guinea or a businessman, yet five years down the line he is driving me around and telling me quite openly what he is doing. He was proud in Papua New Guinea and he is proud in Australia.

Australia is a big, big country but unfortunately they still have a very confined methodology and they continue to discriminate against us, their former colony. Countries like France and England do not. The European Union, for instance, still opens up the market for former colonies to have concessions. Australia looks after its refugees better than they do their former colony. At one stage we had only three million people and even then Australia did not open up much for us. Very few Papua New Guineans, even now, would really want to live in Australia because, simply put, we just do not have the capacity to live there. We could stay for a month and we would go broke.

Perhaps Australia is frightened that we will transmit terrible diseases and sometimes that is the approach these white countries use, to stop black people from freely travelling to their part of the world. That is why they pump so much aid and so much publicity about diseases like HIV, whereas malaria, which is the biggest killer, gets bugger all. All we need is good drugs. For a lot of these things, there are wrong reasons behind the decisions. If they became more genuine in their relationship things would be okay.

Australia is very generous with the Chinese, however. The Chinese are also coming to Papua New Guinea, with or without invitation. I am not against the Chinese although earlier in the piece they were very discriminating to my father.

Over the years I have had contact with all the Australian leaders. I had very little to do with Prime Minister Bob Hawke – I had far more contact with Paul Keating and then later John Howard. Paul Keating knew that Papua New Guinea existed, but he always behaved as if he was trying to live with the upper echelon of people,

229

the intellectuals. He tried to get things across by philosophising a lot. He was a fighter in the Australian parliament but to me his feet were never really on the ground. He belonged to that intellectual class or at least he was emulating others so he could be in that class. Keating was quite well informed but he could not really display it; he could not really walk the talk.

When he attended the South Pacific Forum he seemed to fly over these little countries. Although he did not have a strong voice internationally he was going to make it known to the world that everybody should start focussing on Australia. He would talk about bringing the economic co-operation of Asia and he successfully projected the image of Australia as a significant player. Whether it was in a forum or an international meeting, he tried to rub shoulders with the Clintons and people like that, people who philosophised a lot.

Very little really happened between us while he was Prime Minister between 1991 and 1996 because we were talking at different levels and focussed on different issues. I got him to come to Papua New Guinea for the twentieth year of Independence celebrations. We made him a chief and took him to the Kokoda Trail. The Foreign Affairs Minister during this time, Gareth Evans, tried very hard to assimilate himself with the developing world. He did try hard and I liked him a little because he never took any negative position on Papua New Guinea. He never came out strongly or made a very clear commitment on things so he was pretty airy-fairy. Gareth Evans was more of an international expert and he tried to interpret Papua New Guinea as among one of those developing countries of the world.

They say that John Howard was a political master but to me he was just really a bureaucrat. He thought bureaucratically and he did things administratively to the letter of the law. I did not think he would deviate from a narrow path or think of something that was out of the ordinary. I did not think he was very imaginative. He stuck to the status quo and he was down to earth. He liked to bowl the cricket ball and turn up for football and enjoy it. He did the right thing all the time. I do not think he would ever take any risks. We conversed, we smiled at each other, but not often. I could not say he was my friend and I do not think he liked me very much either because I stood my ground over the Sandline affair. It may be that he expected me to listen more to the Australian side of things – I committed the gravest offence when I failed to listen to Australia at the time of the crisis. He presumed that I should.

I thought by the time of the Sandline crisis that Papua New Guinea had paid back sufficient recognition to Australia and Australia had definitely benefitted from the relationship in terms of their advantages in mines across the country. At what point we should feel that we had compensated each other I did not know, but I was not ready to compromise the independence of Papua New Guinea. Howard was still operating in the paternalistic vein of the former colonial power – that was something I did not subscribe to any longer. I had gone past that. I believed I was just as much a master of my own destiny as Howard.

Maybe he was a very exact and comprehensive person but he never invented things. He inherited a better system in Australia – I made it in Papua New Guinea. I helped construct this country. My vision for Papua New Guinea was completely different from his vision of governance. That is the best way I can describe it.

I like to think I invented the currency, I invented the Central Bank, and I fulfilled the promises I made to the people that we were going to spread the banks right throughout the country. You could say that a lot of us were inventors and we were taking this country forward. I was not going to allow an honorary politician with the same inherited school of thought and opinion to come and just knock me like that.

What can Australia learn from Papua New Guinea? Probably the art of sharing. Papua New Guineans have greater right to access to Australia than any other people. In Port Moresby the Australian High Commission office is totally barricaded and dominated by its intelligence network. They are not making things easier, they are making things tougher for us. They seem to have a very irresponsible, totally biased and discriminatory attitude.

I know other people talk about coming to a point in life where you have done all you can, but I do not think you can ever reach that point. If there is a little entry into a way of doing things you should always exhaust it. It is a simple question of: if I do not do it who will? I like to do things because they are hard to do. I am redeveloping the stabilisation scheme now for copra and cocoa – I did it before but it waned and that is one way of distributing all the royalties from the mine. I suppose it will come to a point when I cannot think of any more things to do. That is probably when I will call it a day.

One of my strengths is that I have always been determined to do what I feel is right. If you work with me and I happen to be the captain, then you just have to do it the way I think is right and if you do not, the greatest thing about democracy is that you are free to go. I have always lived like that. Once a person even mentions that something might be a little bit hard, I tell them, 'It is time. You move on so I can continue to put this policy in place in the way it should be.'

One disease we will never be able to cure is getting old. I feel I am somewhat handicapped by the kind of activity I used to do before. I have always been a very sporty character and I always want to be on the move. I have tried to be faster than anybody, fitter than all, do more than any others and command things. I felt older after I lost office in 1997, and when I was ten years out in the wilderness. I began to feel that my memory was starting to get a little slow. It was good that I was able to get back and start to activate my mind and my brain. However, I know I am not thinking as fast as I should and sometimes I forget. About ten years ago, I was able to pin a speech that I made at a particular point, on that specific date, right there. I cannot do that so easily anymore.

My mind now is almost solely focussed on New Ireland. When I am not in control of a situation, I do not pretend I can influence it, so it is better for me not to worry about it and just concentrate on the things I am capable of doing. It is no good talking about victory if you are not a player in a game. Experience has taught me what I can influence. That is probably what age has taught me over time.

I tell everybody in New Ireland that my government operates in the same way as the Holy Trinity. This is the way I have explained it to them – it needs all the arms of the government to function.

'My political arm, because you elected me, I am the Father. Then the Son is the administration, and the Holy Spirit is you. With all three of us working closely together, it will be the Holy Trinity and that will make New Ireland move forward.'

Nobody is going to question that. That is a complete philosophy.

The future for me at this point in my life is that I know my limitations and I know I have to stay fit to survive the times. I will do what I can in the physical world to keep myself active but I have no desire to compete with anybody. In a way I have established myself and I can live the rest of my life comfortably.

My greatest satisfaction is probably that I have done my best under the circumstances, in whatever time, in whatever situation, I have given the best I could and I am still working now as hard as I worked 40 years ago.

I seem to sometimes forget the roots of where the country began. That was very important in terms of the vision of what we started at Independence but time moves on. I would be quite happy to leave that decade to survive on its own. Historians may wish to look at it but I will not be around to debate with them. Looking back, I am able to put that early stage away into a place I feel very contented with. It was an enormous privilege to be part of the founding of this nation.

I have never really attempted to possess the position I was privileged to hold; the good thing about that is that I have risen and fallen several times so I have always been able to keep my feet on the ground. Other people like Michael Somare would find the relinquishing of power very, very hard; he has to take everybody with him. He cannot live a normal life anymore. I am able to, I can just forget about everything.

I am looking now at a lot of people getting very old and hope I will be like them when I reach that age. I will simply go on until nature itself completely exhausts every piece of blood and bone in my body and then I will call it a day. If I stop now I will probably kick the bucket. I stopped for ten years and I began to get slower but my mind is very active at the moment. I am sending messages, guiding my office, and they have a briefing for me every day. It is the mental activity that makes me forget about my physical weakness and my age. I just behave the way I have always done and only nature will take it away from me. One day it will say, 'Enough, gone, finish now, your time is up.' It is a dreadful thought.

I do not think we can imagine what happens after death. If there is a judgement I want to be judged on the better side of me. I want to be judged that on this planet I was human and on the good things I have done. And on the bad things? I believe you can forgive, not seven times but seventy times seven. That is what I hope.

I have always had a very close relationship with the sea from the time I was a baby, and right through my adult life. In every place I live in now, the sea is right next to me. I have to look at the sea, to have water near me all the time. In Kavieng, at Huris and Port Moresby there is always the sea in front of me. It is probably the vastness of being in a place where you can look at the horizon, to the end of the world, you might say, that makes me feel infinite.

Why is it important to me? It is probably the destiny of the unknown, the world beyond, like the world of self-government and independence. We could not see it; we could not touch it. If I could have seen the future, then I would have had nothing to fight for. Because I could not see it, I could not see victory or defeat. It was that world of adventure that we went into and we just had to keep going.

If a person meets fortune, they are lucky. If they meet misfortune, as a lot of us do sometimes, then that is what life is all about. A person cannot just be stationary in life, they have to be mobile and, because they do not know where they are going, they just have to go. If they were able to predict, it would lower their ability and the strength to want to get there. People build as they go, and I like to think that I too have been a creator in my own life and in the early life of my country.

When I die, I will be buried back at home. It is serene, quiet and it depicts my whole life. Generally I am not a very sociable kind of person and I like a little bit of time on my own in everything I do. I work very hard during the day but at night time I just want to be alone. I like to catch up with myself and go to sleep when I want to. I have always wanted to be able to dictate my own life. Where nobody is, that is my home.

In a hundred years from now that is where you can come and visit me. By the sea, at Huris.

ACKNOWLEDGEMENTS

I would first like to acknowledge my immediate family. Thanks must go to my wife, Stella, whose loyalty and dedication to our family have provided me with a network of unfailing support, and to my children, Vanessa, Byron, Mark and Toea, whose formative years were often without intimate fatherly care due to my parliamentary duties.

My gratitude also extends to my very reliable younger brother Michael, his family, my siblings, grandchildren, cousins and extended family, Piglem Clan, the people of New Ireland, and PPP supporters throughout PNG.

I would like to give thanks to my fellow former Prime Ministers, Sir Michael Somare, Paias Wingti, Sir Rabbie Namaliu, and Sir Mekere Morauta.

I also acknowledge Sir Henry ToRobert, Ross Garnaut, Gerea Aipi, Koiari Tarata and many others whose efforts contributed towards the building of our nation.

I would like to thank all my dedicated, hardworking staff who have had careers lasting more than forty years. I include

Warren Dutton, Hudson Arek, Bruce and Monica Harris, the late John Maneke, Sir Ken Tresize, Brigadier-General Ted Diro, and Henao Rarua.

I also commend all my loyal staff members for their devotion and hard work.

I am grateful to all my drivers, security guards and dedicated liaison and general workers, especially my Highlander watchmen, in particular Andrais and Jimmy from Simbai – both guardians of my house now buried at Manmantinut.

I would like to acknowledge the pioneers of my political career, including Dick Lanzarote, Xavier Han, ToMaibe Rongtui, and Wesley Haririan. I am also very grateful to the chiefs, coastwatchers, and their relatives.

Thanks must go to all the reliable and hardworking housekeepers who have kept me out of the kitchen and laundry.

I am indebted to my writer and editor, former Papua New Guinea correspondent and journalist Lucy Palmer. Her creative vision, diligence, professionalism, and passion for PNG culture and history have made this memoir possible.

I would also like to thank those who have contributed to the creation of this book, including Adam Vai Delaney, Kylie Matthews, the Memoir Makers, Frances O'Connor and Joanne Holliman. I am grateful for the team at UQP, including Cathy Vallance, Madonna Duffy, Greg Bain, Sally Belford and Rachel Crawford, for their professionalism and vision.

INDEX